SCIENCE

Everyday Electricity

HERON BOOKS
K-12 CURRICULUM

At Heron Books, we think learning should be engaging and fun. It should be hands-on and it should allow students to move at their own pace.

For this purpose, we have created an accompanying learning guide to help the student progress through this book, chapter by chapter, with increasing confidence, interest and independence.

Get your free learning guide at *heronbooks.com/learningguides*.

For a final exam, email *teacherresources@heronbooks.com*.

We would love to hear from you!
Email us at *feedback@heronbooks.com*.

Published by
Heron Books, Inc.
20950 SW Rock Creek Road
Sheridan, OR 97378

heronbooks.com

———————

Special thanks to all the teachers and students who provided feedback instrumental to this edition.

———————

IN THIS BOOK

This books contains a
FREE LEARNING GUIDE

Name _____   Start date _____

Learning Guide

PART 1

1. Read *Five Senses*, Chapter 1 Our Senses.   _____

2. ACTIVITY Make a sketchbook to use on this course.

   ☐ Get 7 pieces of blank paper and fold them in half.

   ☐ Make a cover using a piece of construction paper of whatever color you like.

   ☐ Get some help stapling the pages and cover together.   _____

PART 2

1. Read Chapter 2 Sight.   _____

2. ACTIVITY Look at your eyes in a mirror.

   ☐ Notice the pupil and the iris.

   ☐ Close both eyes for a while. When you open them, look to see if your pupils get larger or smaller.   _____

Download and print more copies at
www.heronbooks.com/learningguides

Additional Resources

A **materials list** for the learning guide is at the back of this book.

For an **exam and answers**, email *teacherresources@heronbooks.com*.

Everyday Electricity

Name _____ Date _____

PURPOSE

Find out what electricity is,
where it comes from, and how to work with it.

HOW TO DO THIS COURSE: Do the steps in order. Write your initials and the date on the sign-off line when you finish a step. Two lines means you get the step checked by another student or, if stated, by your teacher. Have them initial the second line. All written work is turned in to your teacher.

ESTIMATED TIME: 15 hours.

BOOK:

Everyday Electricity, Heron Books

A. ATOMS AND ELECTRICITY

1. READ: *Everyday Electricity*, Chapter 1 Electricity. _____

2. ACTIVITY: Look around and see how many things you can find that use electricity. _____

3. READ: Chapter 2 Atoms and How They Work, to the section, "Protons, Neutrons and Electrons." _____

4. ACTIVITY: Use objects to show an atom with its electrons and nucleus (show the parts of the nucleus). ____ ____

5. READ: Chapter 2, section "Protons, Neutrons and Electrons." _____

6. ACTIVITY: Use objects to show electrical force.

☐ between two electrons

☐ between two protons

☐ between one proton and one electron _____

7. READ: Chapter 2, section "Free Electrons." _____

8. ACTIVITY: Balloon Experiment.

For this activity you will need

- two small balloons
- a piece of string about two feet long

☐ Blow up and tie the balloons, being careful not to let them rub on your shirt or sweater.

☐ Tie one balloon to each end of the string.

☐ Hold the balloons up by the middle of the string and observe how they hang.

☐ Now rub the balloons on your shirt or sweater. This causes free electrons to move from the cloth to the balloons.

☐ Hold the balloons up again and observe how they hang now.

☐ Tell your teacher what you observed and how electrical force could explain this.

Teacher pass _____ _____

9. ACTIVITY: Styrofoam Experiment.

For this activity you will need

- a piece of string about two feet long
- two small Styrofoam balls
- one small balloon

☐ Get a small balloon, blow it up and tie it.

☐ Tie one Styrofoam ball to each end of the string.

☐ Hold the string in the middle so the Styrofoam balls hang down. Observe how they hang.

☐ Rub the balloon on your shirt or sweater.

☐ Hold the balloon next to the Styrofoam (don't let it touch) and observe what happens.

☐ Now touch the balloon to the Styrofoam balls and observe what happens.

☐ Tell your teacher what you observed and how electrical force could explain this.

Teacher pass   _____ _____

10. ACTIVITY: Water Experiment.

For this activity you will need

- one small balloon

- a water faucet

☐ Blow up the balloon and tie it.

☐ Rub the balloon on your shirt or sweater as you did in the earlier experiments. Hold the balloon while you do the next step. Don't put it down.

☐ Run a narrow stream of cold water from a faucet. The stream should be about as wide as a pencil.

☐ Hold the balloon close to the stream of water but don't let it touch.

☐ Observe what happens to the water.

☐ Tell your teacher what you saw, and how electrical force could explain this.

Teacher pass   _____ _____

B. WHAT IS ELECTRICITY?

1. READ: Chapter 3 What Is Electricity? _____

2. ACTIVITY: Use objects to show how positive protons, negative electrons and electrical force create electrical current. _____

3. ACTIVITY: Look around and find at least five things that could be conductors and five that could be insulators. **Teacher pass** ____ - ____

4. READ: Chapter 4 Electrical Circuits, to the heading "Strong Current and Weak Current." _____

5. ACTIVITY: Make a Circuit.

   For this activity you will need

   - one 6-volt battery
   - one 6-volt miniature light bulb
   - one light bulb socket
   - one knife switch
   - three alligator clip wires

   ☐ Use the battery, wires, light bulb, switch and socket to create a circuit.

   ☐ Open and close the switch several times and watch what happens to the bulb. _____

6. READ: Chapter 4, sections "Strong Current and Weak Current" and "A 'Law' About Electrons." _____

7. ACTIVITY: Voltage and Resistance.

    For this activity you will need

    - two 6-volt batteries
    - two 6-volt miniature light bulbs
    - two light bulb sockets
    - four alligator clip wires

    ☐ Make a circuit with one 6-volt battery and one light
      bulb. Observe how bright the bulb is.

    ☐ Increase the resistance in the circuit by adding another
      bulb. Observe how bright the bulb is.

    ☐ Now increase the voltage in the circuit by adding
      another 6-volt battery. Observe how bright the bulb is.

    ☐ Explain to another person what you observed and how
      this demonstrates Ohm's law.   ____ ____

8. READ: Chapter 4, section "Short Circuits."   _____

9. ACTIVITY: Make a Short Circuit.

    For this activity you will need

    - one 6-volt battery
    - one 6-volt miniature light bulb
    - one light bulb socket
    - two alligator clip wires
    - aluminum foil

    ☐ Make a circuit with the battery and light bulb.

    ☐ Cut a strip of aluminum foil about one inch wide and
      three inches long.

☐ Fold the aluminum foil lengthwise several times so that you have a narrow strip of foil about three inches long.

☐ Use the foil strip to connect the wires that are attached to the bulb to each other.

☐ Observe what happens to the bulb.

☐ Notice how the aluminum feels.

☐ Explain to another person what you observed and what happened to the electrons in this circuit.   _____ _____

10. READ: Chapter 5 Electrical Wires   _____

11. ACTIVITY: Get samples of different kinds of wire from your teacher.

☐ Read the labels on each wire that say what they are for.

☐ Notice the thickness of each wire and how much insulation each has.

☐ Bend each wire to see how flexible it is.

☐ Work out which wire is made to handle the most current and voltage, and which is made to handle the least.

☐ In writing, explain what you decided and why.   _____ _____

12. ACTIVITY: Look around and find at least ten things with different kinds of electrical wiring. For each one, notice what the wire is supplying power to and how thick the wire is.   _____

C. HOW ELECTRICITY IS PRODUCED

1. READ: Chapter 6 How Electricity is Produced, to the heading "Power Stations."   _____

2. ACTIVITY: Make a Vinegar Battery.

For this activity you will need

- vinegar
- five nails wrapped with wire
- plastic ice cube tray
- One LED bulb

☐ Fill six sections of the ice cube tray with vinegar.

☐ Place the wires and nails in the tray as shown in the picture below. Make sure the wire from one nail doesn't touch the next nail.

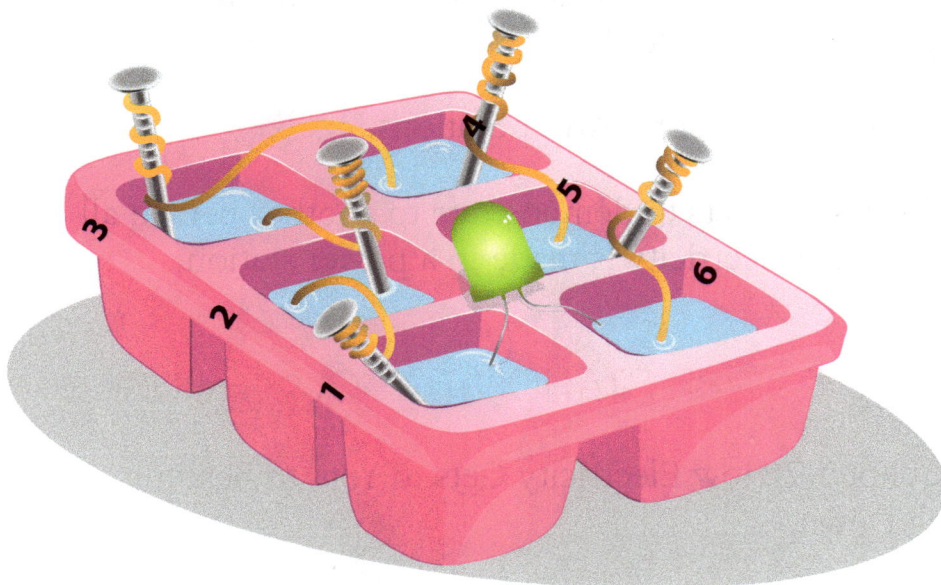

☐ Place the LED light with one wire in the first section and the other in the last section. Observe what happens to the bulb.

Remember that vinegar is a chemical. It combines with the metal in the nails and wires to create free electrons that move through the wires and light the bulb.

3. ACTIVITY: Make Electric Current with a Magnet and Wire.

For this activity you will need

- a galvanometer (a device that measures electric current)

- a three-inch-long bolt wrapped with wire

- a magnet

☐ Attach the ends of the wire on the bolt to the galvanometer.

☐ Move the magnet back and forth next to the wire and watch the needle on the galvanometer. Then move the wire back and forth near the magnet. Watch what happens to the needle. _____

4. READ: Chapter 6, section "Power Stations." _____

5. ACTIVITY: Use objects to demonstrate to another person all the steps of how electricity is made in a power station. ____ ____

D. FROM THE POWER STATION TO YOUR HOUSE

1. READ: Chapter 7 How Electricity Gets to You, to heading "Stepping Down." _____

2. ACTIVITY: Use a Transformer to Change Voltage.

For this activity you will need

- a transformer that can step 120 volts down to 9 to 12 volts

- one 6-volt miniature light bulb (this type of bulb can take up to 12 volts for a short period of time)

- a voltmeter (this is a device that measures voltage)

- two alligator clip wires

☐ With your teacher helping, use the voltmeter to measure the voltage coming from a wall outlet. Write the voltage here ____. Decide whether your light bulb can handle that voltage and tell your teacher.

☐ Plug the transformer into the wall outlet.

☐ With your teacher helping, measure the voltage coming from the transformer. Write the voltage here ____. Decide whether your light bulb can handle that voltage and tell your teacher.

☐ Use the alligator clip wires to connect your 6-volt light bulb to the wires coming from the transformer. See what happens.

Teacher pass   ____ ____

3. READ: Chapter 7, from section "Stepping Down" to heading "Safety."   _____

4. ACTIVITY: Use objects to demonstrate for another person all the steps of electricity getting from a power station to a neighborhood. Be sure to show the voltage changes along the way.   ____ ____

5. ACTIVITY:

☐ Look at several different outdoor power lines.

☐ For each one you see, count the insulators between the power line and the pole or pylon.

☐ Make a list of the power lines you look at and how many insulators each one has. On your list, say which power line you think has the most voltage and which one you think has the least and why you think this.   ____ ____

6. READ: Chapter 7, section "Safety" to the end of the chapter.   _____

E. ELECTRICITY IN YOUR HOUSE

1. READ: Chapter 8 Electricity in Your House, to the heading "Circuit Box." _____

2. ACTIVITY: Find the electric meter that measures power coming into the building you are in. _____

3. READ: Chapter 8, section "Circuit Box" to the end of the chapter. _____

4. ACTIVITY: Do this activity with an adult. At your home or school, look at the main circuit box.

   ☐ Find the master switch.

   ☐ By counting all the circuit breakers, see how many circuits the power is split into. _____ _____

5. ACTIVITY: Get a circuit breaker from your teacher and look it over. Switch it off and on. _____

6. READ: Chapter 9 Circuits in Your House, to the heading "House Circuits." _____

7. ACTIVITY: Build Series and Parallel Circuits.

   For this activity you will need
   - two 6-volt mini light bulbs
   - two bulb sockets
   - one 6-volt battery
   - four alligator clip wires

   ☐ Make a circuit with the battery and one light bulb. Observe how bright the bulb is.

   ☐ Now add another bulb in a series circuit. Notice how bright the bulbs are now.

☐ Remove one of the bulbs. What happens to the other bulb?

☐ Rewire your circuit so that both bulbs are connected in a parallel circuit. What do you notice about the brightness of the bulbs?

☐ Remove one of the bulbs from your parallel circuit. What happens to the other bulb?

☐ Show your teacher your parallel circuit, and explain what you observed from doing this activity.

Teacher pass _____ _____

8. READ: Chapter 9, section "House Circuits" to the end of the chapter. _____

9. ACTIVITY: If possible, find the place where the safety ground for your home or school is connected to the actual ground. Look at how it is connected. _____

10. ACTIVITY: Look at the picture of a complete circuit at the end of the chapter.

☐ Find the hot, neutral and ground wires.

☐ With your finger, trace the path of electric current from the circuit box, through the outlets, switch and light, and back to the circuit box. Notice how the light and each outlet get power from the circuit without breaking the path of the current. _____

11. READ: Chapter 10 Outlets and Plugs. _____

12. ACTIVITY: Look at different outlets and plugs. See which plugs have a ground wire prong and what they are connected to. Write down several things you noticed. _____ _____

F. PUTTING IT TOGETHER

1. READ: Chapter 11 Everyday Electricity.   _____

2. ACTIVITY: Make a diagram that shows the full path of how
   electricity gets from a power station to the refrigerator in your
   home. Be sure to show how voltage changes along the way.
   (Save your diagram for the exam.) **Teacher pass**   ____ ____

3. ACTIVITY:

   ☐ Look around your school, your neighborhood and
      your home and make a list of at least 15 things that
      direct or use electricity.

   ☐ For each item on your list, say where you think the
      electricity comes from and what is being done with it.

   Teacher pass   ____ ____

4. ACTIVITY: Produce Electricity Yourself.

   You have seen that electricity can be produced by moving a
   magnet near a wire. In this activity you will use this idea to
   produce electricity yourself.

   For this activity you will need

   - small motor that has been opened so the inside can be
     seen.

   - small hand-operated generator

   - alligator clip wires

   - several light bulbs and motors

   ☐ Get a small motor that has been opened so you can
      see inside it. Notice there are some magnets around
      the inside of the motor. Also notice that between the
      magnets there are some wires that can be turned.

☐ Get a small hand-operated generator and see how it works. Experiment with the generator to make the light bulb shine.

☐ On the front of the generator there are terminals where wires can be attached. Use alligator clip wires to create a parallel circuit that can power several devices at once. For example, the light on the generator and several other lights or motors.

☐ Show your teacher your parallel circuit and explain how the generator makes electricity to power the devices.

Teacher pass   _____ _____

I have completed the steps of this course. I understand what I studied and can use it.

Student _____ Date _____

The student has completed the steps of this course and knows and can apply what was studied.

Teacher _____ Date _____

The student has passed the exam for this course.

Examiner _____ Date _____

FOR TEACHERS

NOTE:
This course assumes the student knows the information covered in *Light Bulbs, Switches and Batteries*.

Student should save the diagram from step F2 to take to examiner.

ADDITIONAL RESOURCES
Everyday Electricity Teacher Tips
Materials list
Exam and answers

Electricity

Electricity does work for us. We use it in many, many ways every day. It makes light bulbs shine, vacuum cleaners go, amusement-park rides spin, and factories run.

But what exactly *is* electricity and how do we get it to do these things?

To answer these questions we need to know some things about **matter**. Scientists use this word to describe all the things that make up the world around us. Rocks, trees, air, water, animals, dust. These are all matter.

Matter is made up of very, very tiny pieces called **atoms**. There are trillions of atoms in even the smallest speck of dust you can find.

So what does something so tiny have to do with making something as big as a vacuum cleaner run?

Well, atoms are made up of even tinier parts, and to understand what electricity is, you need to know what these are and how they work.

Atoms and How They Work

2

ATOMS

An atom has a center called its **nucleus**, and this is made of tiny parts called **protons** and **neutrons**. The name for a tiny part of an atom is **particle**.

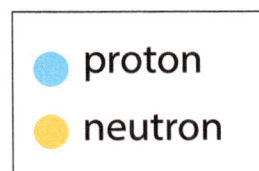

🔵	proton
🟡	neutron

Moving *around* the nucleus are more tiny particles called **electrons**.

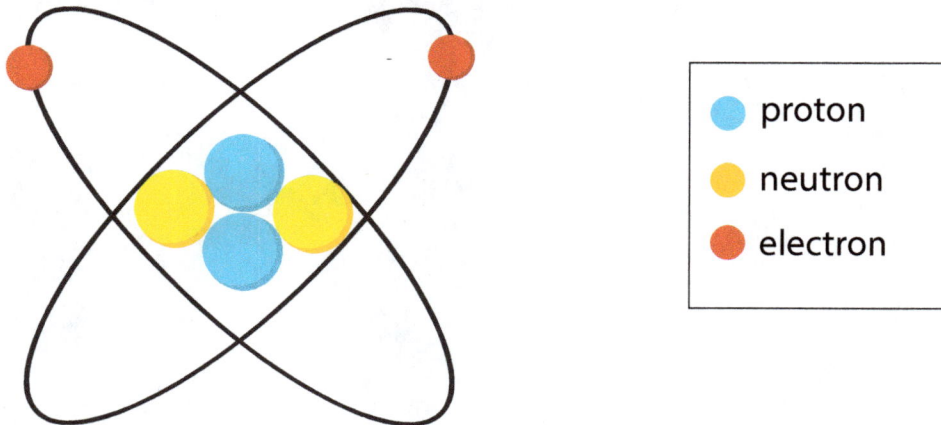

🔵	proton
🟡	neutron
🔴	electron

Atoms have an equal number of protons and electrons.

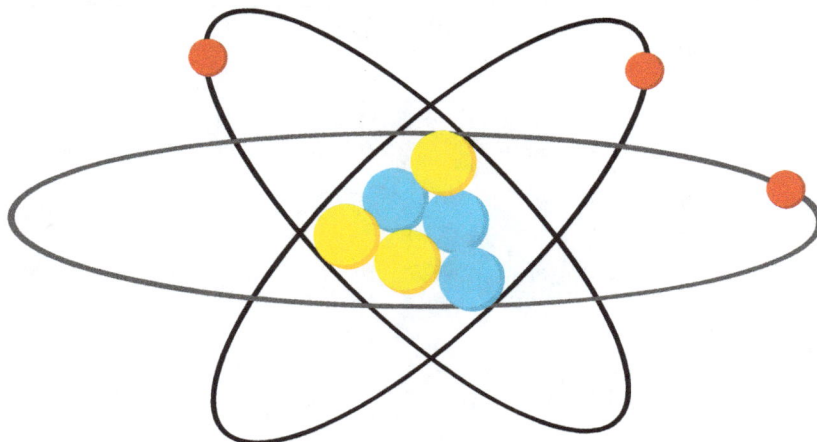

If you could see the atoms in a piece of matter you would see lots of nuclei (NOO klee eye, plural of nucleus). Each one would have some electrons around it.

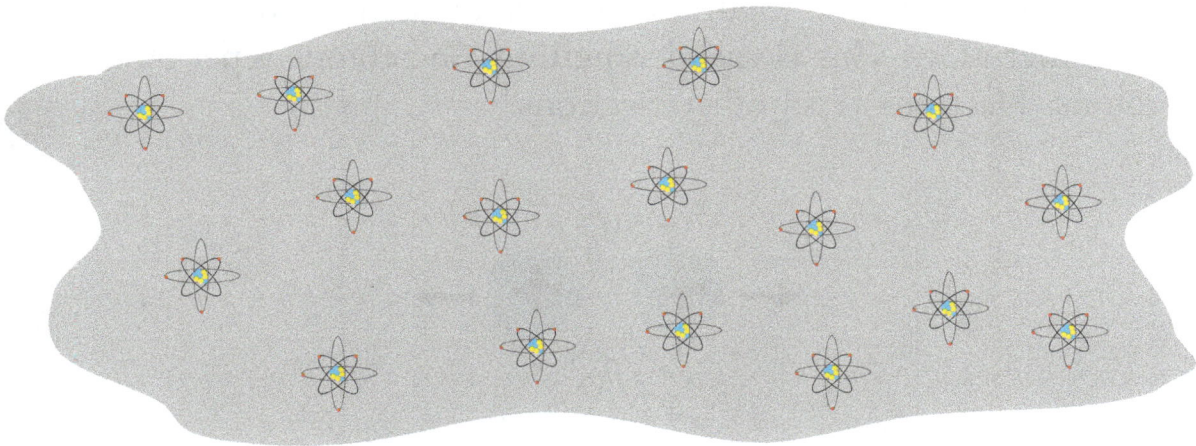

PROTONS, NEUTRONS AND ELECTRONS

When scientists learned about protons, neutrons and electrons, they noticed that they acted in certain ways. They observed, for example, that protons and electrons seemed to be opposites. To show this difference they decided to describe the protons as "positive" and the electrons as "negative." The neutrons they called "neutral," neither positive nor negative.

Electricity has to do with how these particles in atoms act toward one another.

Particles that are alike (both are positive or both are negative) push each other away. This is called **repelling**. So protons repel other protons. Electrons repel other electrons.

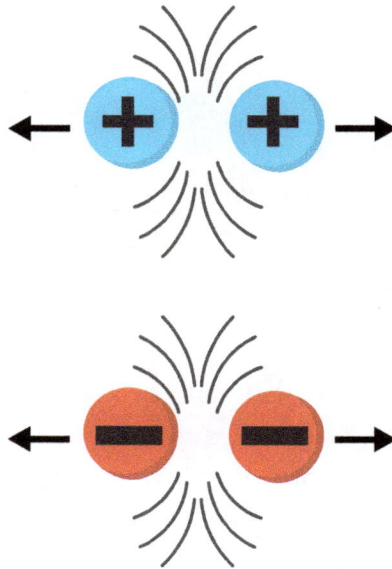

Particles that are opposite (like protons and electrons) pull toward one another. This is called **attracting**. Protons and electrons **attract** one another.

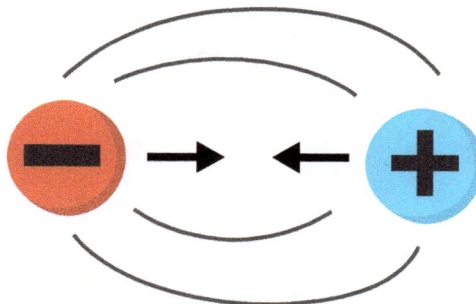

Neutral particles do not push or pull. In other words, they do not repel or attract.

In science, a push or a pull, no matter how weak or strong, is called a **force.** The pulling and the pushing that happens between the particles in an atom has been named **electrical force.**

For example, the tiny pull that happens between an electron and a proton is electrical force. So is the tiny push between proton and proton or between electron and electron.

FREE ELECTRONS

Because the nucleus of an atom is made of positive protons and neutral neutrons, it is overall positive.

Since electrons are negative, they are pulled toward the positive nucleus. The pull is not strong enough to make the electrons stick tight to the nucleus but it is enough to keep them close and moving around it.

In an atom there are just enough negative electrons to balance the positive protons in the nucleus. Because the atom has equal positive and negatives, it is balanced.

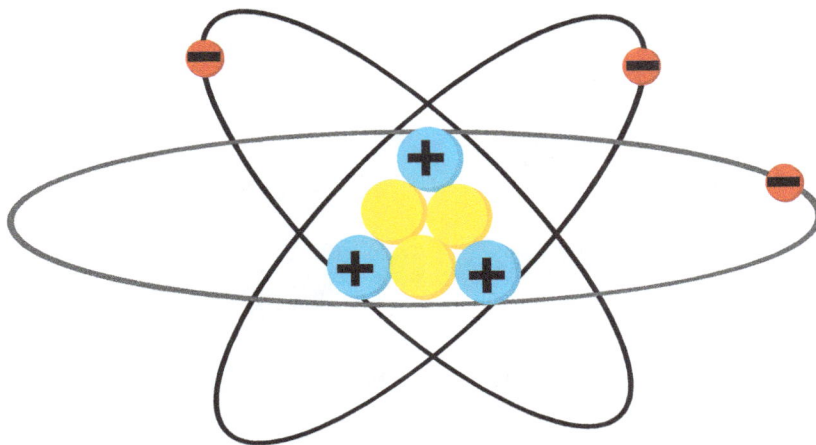

In some kinds of matter, metals for example, the electrons of the atoms are not held as tightly to their nuclei as they are in other kinds of matter. They're a little freer. An electron like this can get away from its nucleus and move from one atom to another. An electron like this is called a **free electron**.

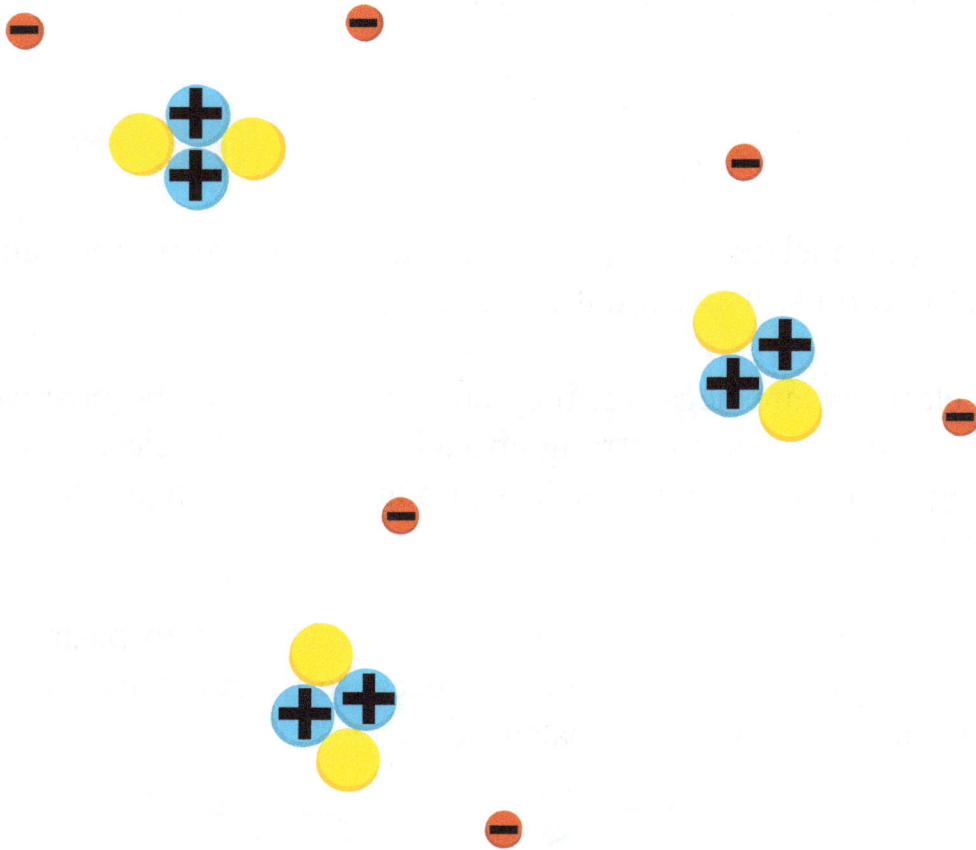

When a free electron moves away from its nucleus, it leaves behind an atom that is not balanced; it is now more positive. So what does the atom do? It attracts another free electron to come to it.

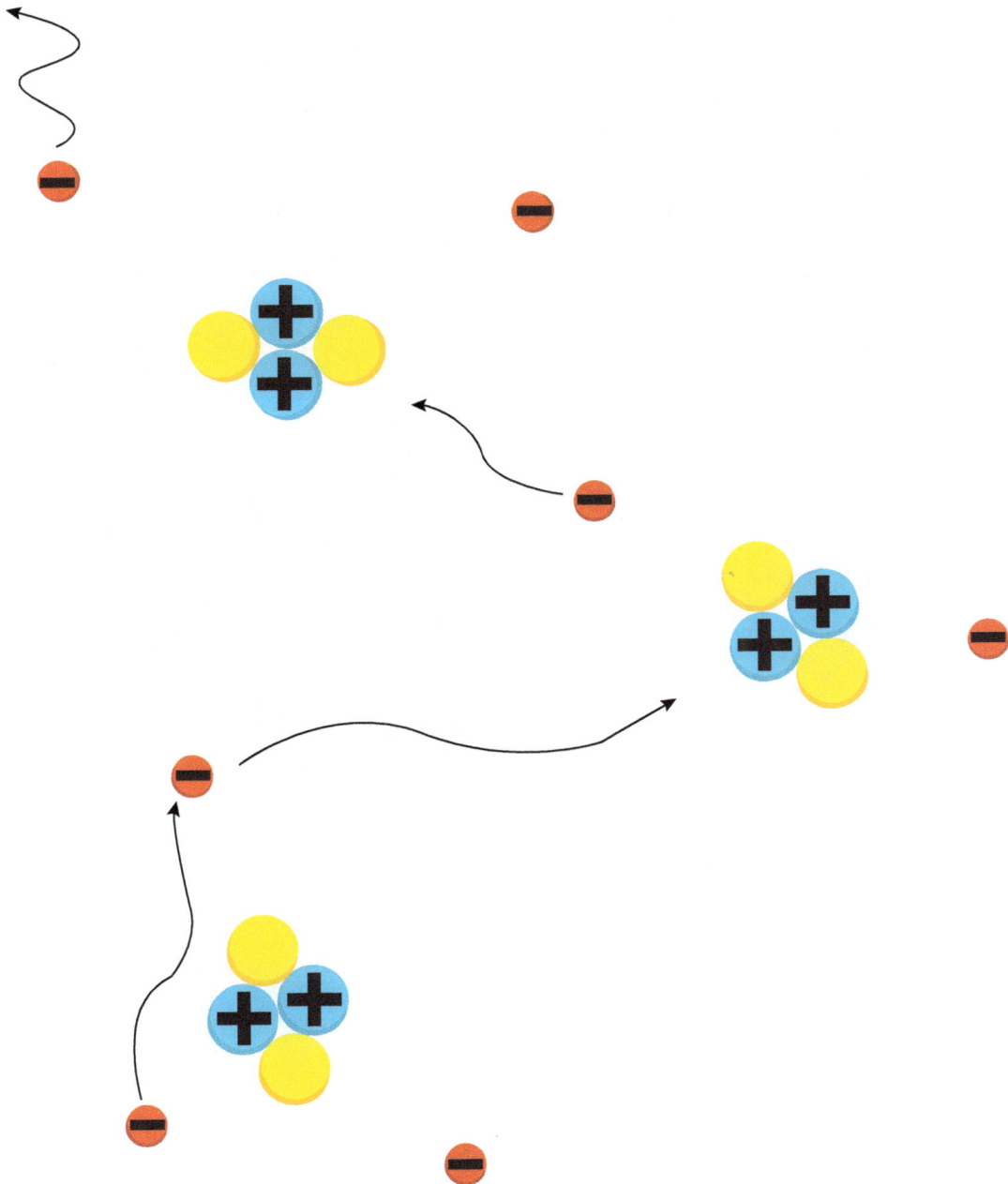

What Is Electricity?

3

Here's how we use all this to create electrical energy for powering things like computers and lights.

Suppose you had two pieces of matter, piece A and piece B. If all the atoms in each piece had an equal number of protons and electrons you could say that each was neutral. Neither one would be more positive or negative.

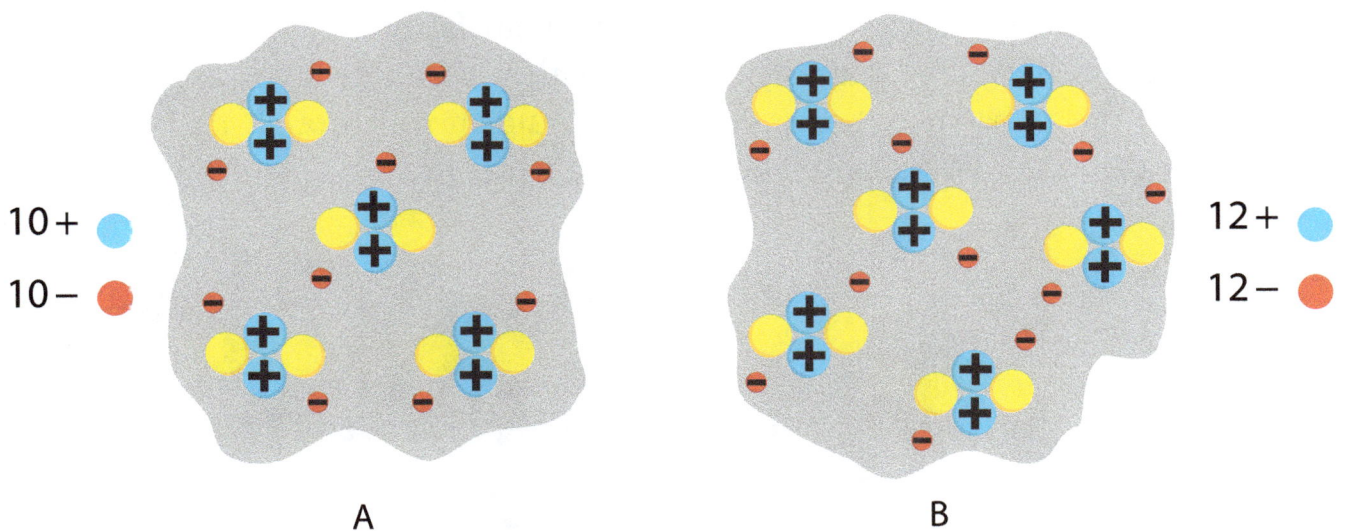

10+ •
10 − •

12+ •
12 − •

A   B

11

Now suppose you were able to move some electrons from piece A to piece B. Now B would have more electrons than protons so the whole piece would be negative. Piece A would have fewer electrons than protons so it would be positive.

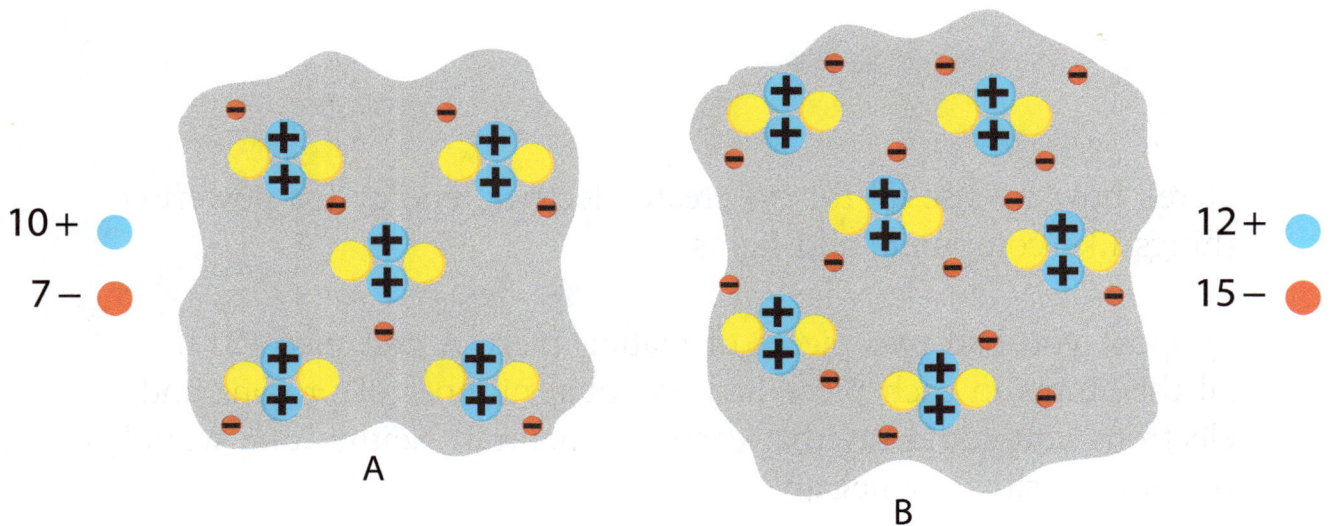

10+ ●
7 − ●

A

12+ ●
15 − ●

B

Metal wires let electrons move through them fairly easily. So if you connected these two pieces of matter with a wire, the two pieces would try to balance. Some electrons would move through the wire from the negative piece to the positive one.

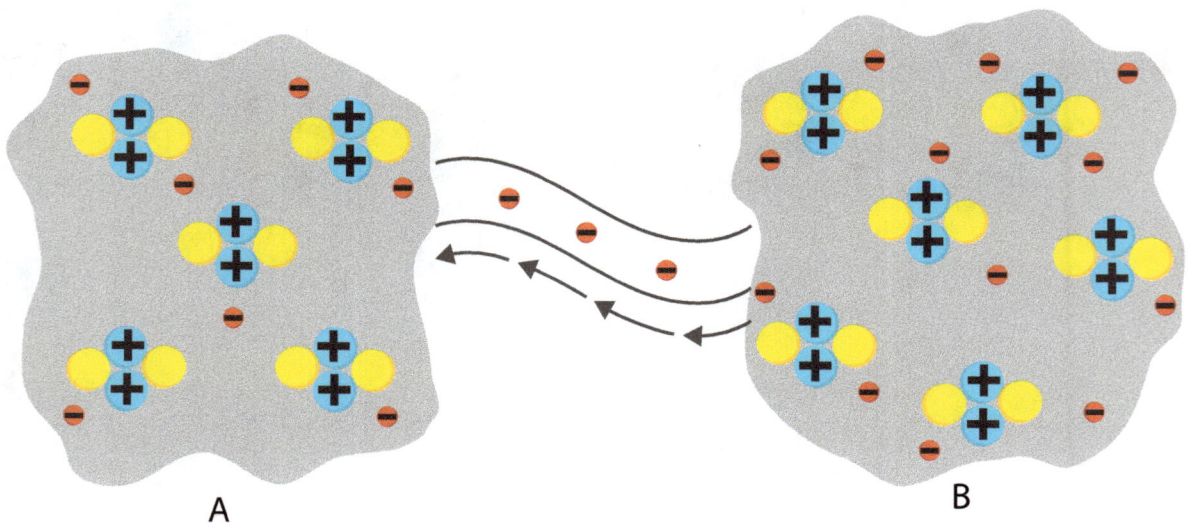

A

B

This is how we get electricity to work for us. We set it up so that free electrons are made to move through wires.

What we call **electricity** is simply the movement of electrons. A lot of moving free electrons can add up to a lot of energy we can use to power things.

ELECTRIC CURRENT

In the atoms of metals, like copper and aluminum, the electrons are not tightly held to the nucleus. They can move more freely. These materials are called **conductors**. They "conduct" electrons— allow them to pass through. Wires made from these metals make an easy path along which electrons can flow.

In other materials, such as glass, plastic, rubber and wood, electrons are held more tightly and don't move around freely. In other words, they can't flow along. These materials are called **insulators** because they don't allow electrons to pass through.

The flow of electrons through a conductor is called **electric current**. To make the current go where we want it to, and keep it from going where we don't want it to go, we use metal wires covered by plastic insulation. The wire lets the current flow and the insulation keeps it in the wire where it belongs. When you touch an electrical wire that's insulated, the insulator keeps the electricity from going into your body.

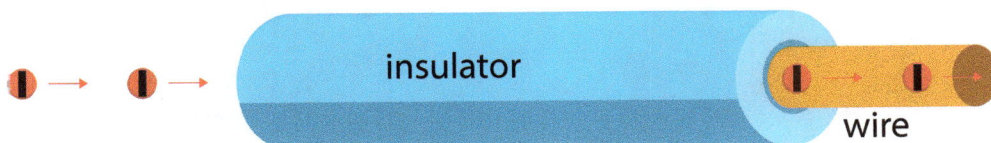

insulator

wire

Electrical Circuits 4

To understand how electricity is used, it can be helpful to know some things about circuits.

A **circuit** is a loop or path that comes back to the same place it starts out. If you start out from your front door, walk around the outside of your house and come back to your front door, you could say that you walked a circuit around your house.

All things that use electricity have to have a way for the electricity to get to them. There has to be a path for the electricity to follow.

An **electrical circuit** is a path for electrons that starts somewhere, for example at a battery, and makes a complete loop back to where it started. This is a picture of a simple circuit with a battery and a light bulb. The electrons leave the battery, travel through the insulated wires and the light bulb, and go back to the other side of battery.

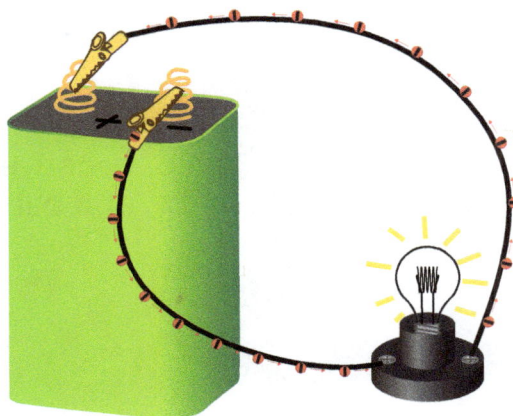

Often a circuit includes a **switch** that can be closed to let electrons flow through the circuit and opened to stop the flow.

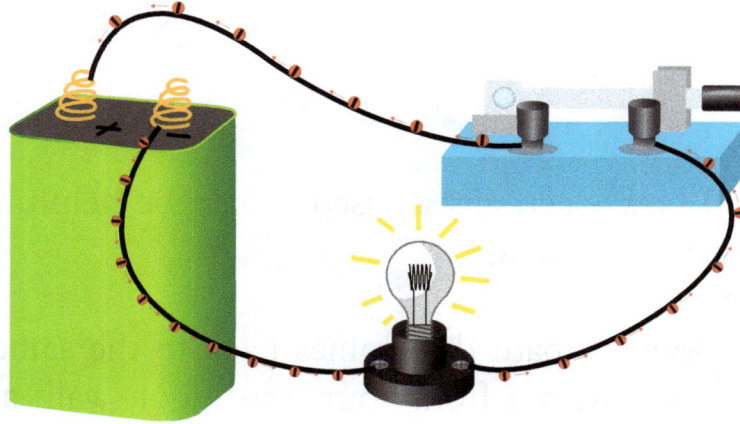

CURRENT IN A CIRCUIT

To make current flow in an electrical circuit, you have to give the electrons a push. Since electrons are negative, they move away from a negative area or towards a positive area. Here's how this works in a battery.

Batteries have two parts. One of the parts has more electrons than protons. It has extra free electrons. This is called the negative part of the battery.

negative part
of a battery

The other part of the battery has more protons than electrons. This is called the positive part of the battery.

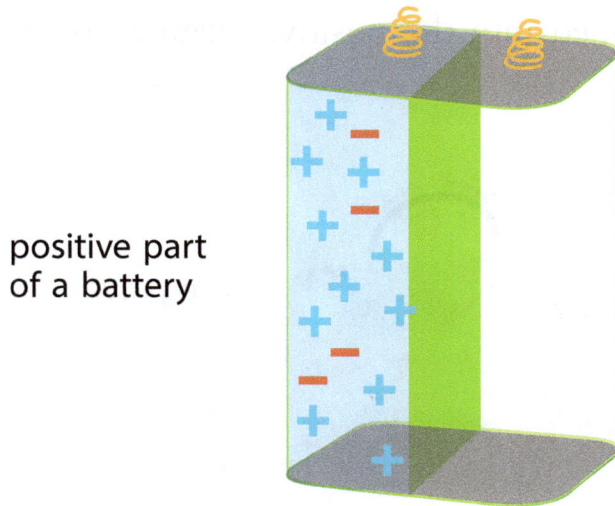

positive part
of a battery

A battery is made so that electrons can't flow from the negative part to the positive part *inside* the battery. This is how a battery stores electrical energy. There are extra free electrons in the negative part waiting to flow to something positive.

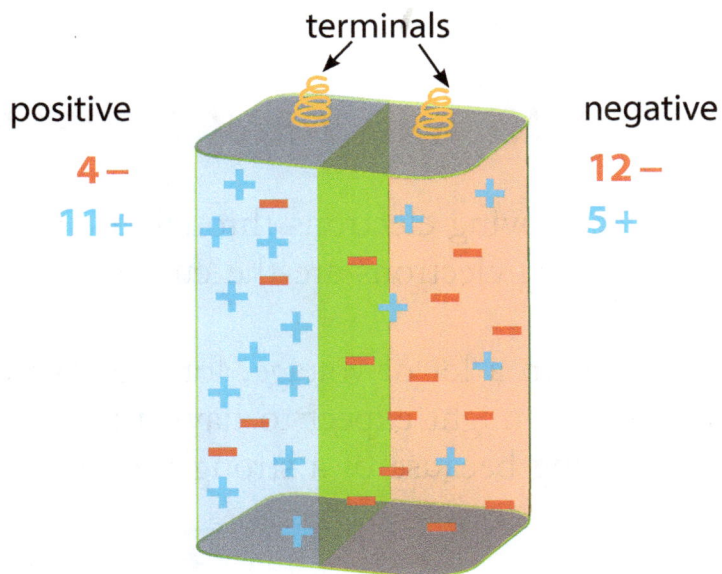

terminals

positive
4 −
11 +

negative
12 −
5 +

Each part of the battery has a place for a wire to connect, called a **terminal**. If you connect the two terminals of a battery with a wire, free electrons will be pushed out of the negative terminal and at the same time pulled into the positive terminal by electrical force.

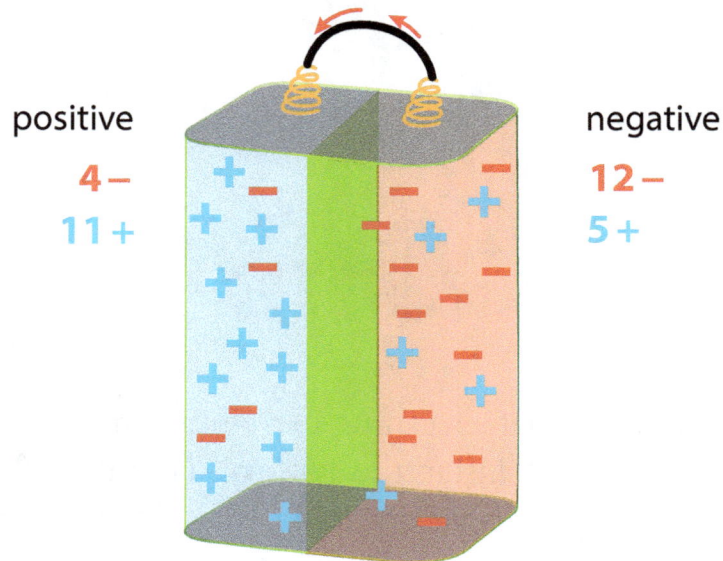

STRONG CURRENT AND WEAK CURRENT

The amount of push moving electrons through a circuit is called the **voltage**. The moving electrons are the current.

If you had a circuit with a lot of voltage, for example one with a very strong battery, you might expect to have a strong current with lots of electrons moving because of a strong electrical force making them move.

However, there is another thing that affects how much current flows in a circuit.

The wires in a circuit make a good path for electrons to flow through. They allow the electrons to move along freely. Other parts of a circuit, for example a light bulb or a motor, don't allow the electrons to move so freely. The electrons have more difficulty moving between the atoms in these things, and are slowed down. This slowing down of the electrons is called **resistance**. Along with voltage, the resistance in a circuit affects how much current can flow in that circuit.

Voltage, resistance and current all relate to one another in an electrical circuit.

To show how, let's start with a circuit that has one battery and one light bulb. The battery provides voltage, the light bulb has resistance, and there is a current of moving electrons. Since the electrons can't move as easily through the light bulb, some of their motion energy is changed into heat energy and light energy. The light bulb shines.

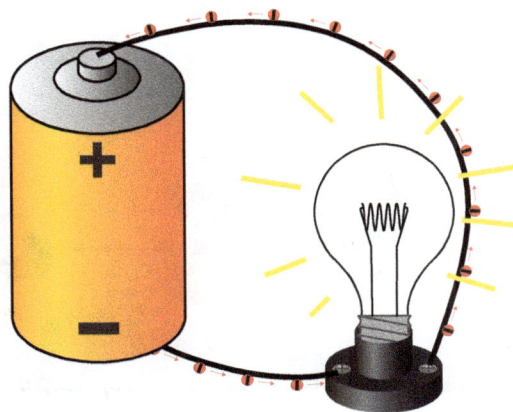

If we increase the *voltage* in this circuit by adding a second battery, there will be more current. Since more electrons are going through the light bulb, they give up more energy in the light bulb. The bulb will get hotter and brighter.

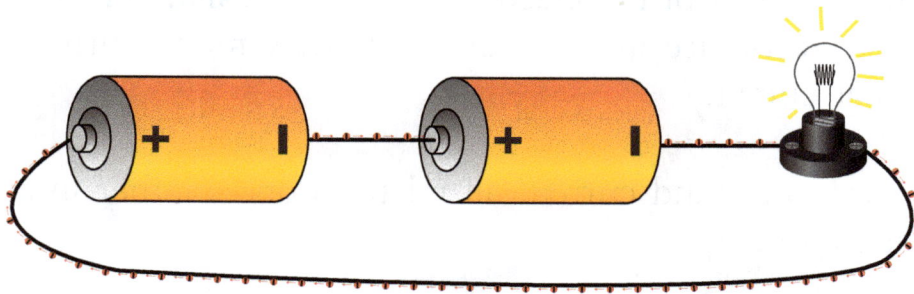

If we increase the *resistance* in the circuit by adding a second light bulb, there will be less current. There will be fewer electrons going through each bulb, so less energy will be used in each one, and they will be dimmer.

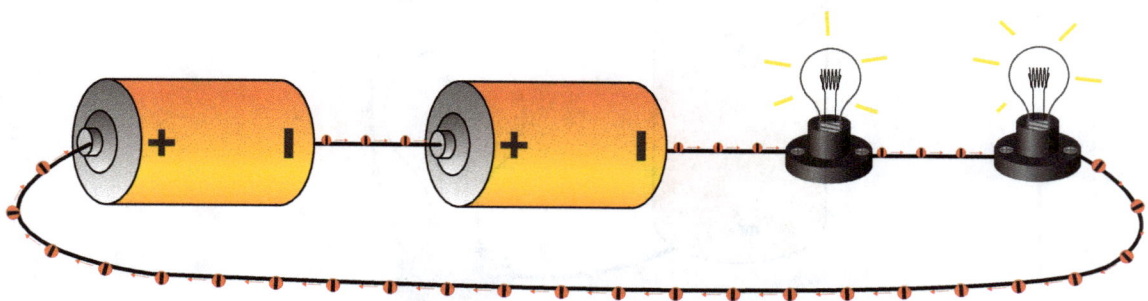

A "LAW" ABOUT ELECTRONS

A **natural law** is a statement about how things act in nature. For example, it is a natural law that when you push a ball on a flat surface, it will keep rolling for a while. Another natural law is that when the sun goes down, it gets dark. In electricity, there is a natural law that describes how voltage, current and resistance are related in an electrical circuit.

This natural law says:

- When voltage is increased, current increases.

- When voltage is decreased, current decreases.

- When resistance is increased, the current decreases.

- When resistance is decreased, the current increases.

This natural law was discovered in 1827 by a German scientist, Georg Ohm, so it is called Ohm's law.

SHORT CIRCUITS

As electrons move through a circuit, they push around and bump among the atoms of the wires. Some of their motion energy gets turned into heat energy. In a circuit that is put together properly this is not a problem. Light bulbs or motors in the circuit provide enough resistance to keep the current at a good level for the wires to manage.

There is a problem with having a circuit that simply connects the two terminals of the battery with nothing in the circuit to provide resistance. In this circuit the electrons flow very quickly from one terminal to the other with nothing to slow them down. A circuit like this is called a **short circuit**. It is a "short" circuit because the electrons are taking a short path between the negative and positive terminals of the battery.

In a circuit like this the wire would probably get very hot. The battery's energy would get used up very quickly because the electrons are flowing very quickly from the negative terminal to the positive terminal. If there was enough current flowing, the wires might get hot enough to melt or cause a fire.

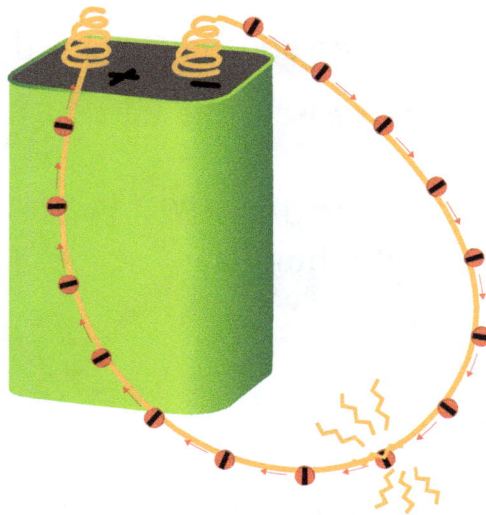

This is another reason that electrical wires have insulation. If you created a circuit with bare wires, and those wires touched each other, it would make an easy path for the electrons to flow through. They would follow this short path rather than flowing through the light bulb. This would be a short circuit. The wires would get hot and perhaps melt.

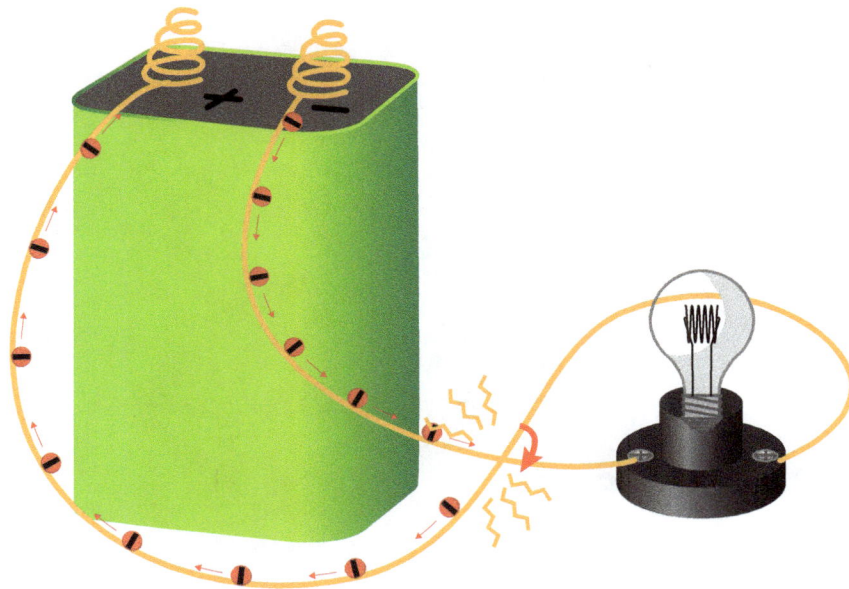

Electrical Wires 5

When you look at things that use electrical energy, like lamps, electric irons and headphones, you see different sizes of wire. Headphone wires are much thinner than lamp cord wires. The cord to an electric iron is thicker than a lamp cord. The wires inside the walls of a building are even thicker. Outside lines that carry power to buildings are very thick. Why are so many different wires needed?

The size of a wire is chosen for how much current it will have to carry and how much voltage is going to be used to push that current along.

HOW MUCH CURRENT?

Although electrical wires allow electrons to flow easily, there is still some resistance. Because of this small amount of resistance, when current flows through a wire some of the electrical energy is changed to heat energy. If there is too much current for the wire to handle, this can also cause it to get very hot and even melt.

How much current will be flowing through a wire determines its size. If there will be a small current, the wire can be very thin. If there will be a lot of current, a thicker wire will be needed. Headphone wires are thin because they carry very little electrical current. Lamps carry more, so their wires are thicker. A wire used to plug in a washing machine is even thicker because it needs to carry a lot more current.

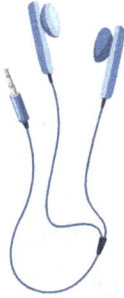

HOW MUCH VOLTAGE?

How much insulation there is on a wire depends on how much voltage the wire will have to handle. Wires used with higher voltages have thicker insulation.

Remember that voltage is how hard the electrons are being pushed or pulled along. If the voltage is high enough, electrons can even pass through an insulator. If you were handling a wire that had a high voltage but too little insulation, the high voltage could cause electrons to move through the insulator, and give your hands a shock. Electrons could also pass through the insulation to another wire and cause a short circuit, which might cause a fire.

low voltage wire

high voltage wire

Voltage is measured in units called **volts**. A flashlight battery provides about 1.5 volts of electrical force. Even if you have two or three batteries hooked together, there is not enough voltage to push much current. Because of this, the wires you use to connect flashlight batteries don't have to be very thick or have much insulation. The insulation they do have is mainly just to keep the wires from touching each other.

The place where you plug in a wire is called an **outlet.** The wall outlets in a house where you plug in a lamp cord provide between 110 and 120 volts of electrical force—about 80 times as much as the flashlight battery. So lamp cords have more insulation. On the other hand, headphone wires have only a fraction of a volt pushing the electrons, so only enough insulation is needed to keep the different wires from touching each other.

WHAT'S THE WIRE USED FOR?

Most wires that carry electrical current have only one wire inside the insulation. However, there is one kind of wire that has many thin metal wires twisted together instead of just one wire. These thin wires are called **strands**, and wire made of many strands twisted together is called **stranded wire**. All of the strands together act as a single conductor.

Stranded wire is used where the wires have to be flexible, because stranded wire is easy to bend and can be bent many times without breaking. For example, a lamp cord or an extension cord may need to be rolled up and unrolled or moved around many times. They are usually made of stranded wire so this can be done without breaking the wire.

solid wire

stranded wire

How Electricity Is Produced

6

We constantly use electricity, but where do we get it? When we need electrical energy we generally use a battery or we plug a cord into a wall outlet. But how does a battery create electrical energy? Where does the electricity that we get from a wall outlet come from?

ELECTRICITY FROM BATTERIES

A battery uses chemicals to produce electricity.

A **chemical** is a material that causes a change in another material when they are combined. For example, baking soda is a chemical. So is vinegar. When baking soda and vinegar are combined they are changed, and bubbles are formed.

A battery contains chemicals that combine with each other in a way that extra electrons end up in one part of the battery and too few electrons in the other. When the battery is then placed in a circuit, the free electrons travel from the negative terminal to the positive terminal, passing through whatever is in the circuit.

9

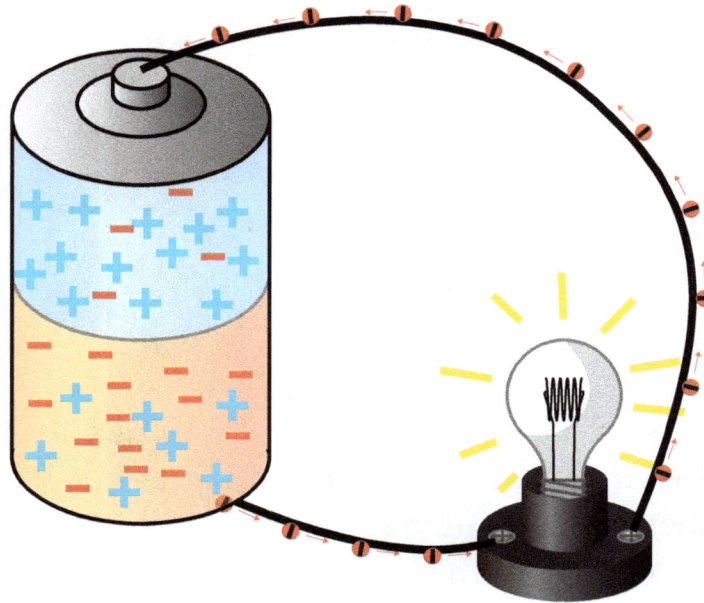

When all the extra electrons from the negative side of the battery have gone over to the positive side, there is no more electrical force pushing or pulling the electrons through the circuit. We say that the battery is "dead" or has no more charge (**charge** is another word for electrical energy).

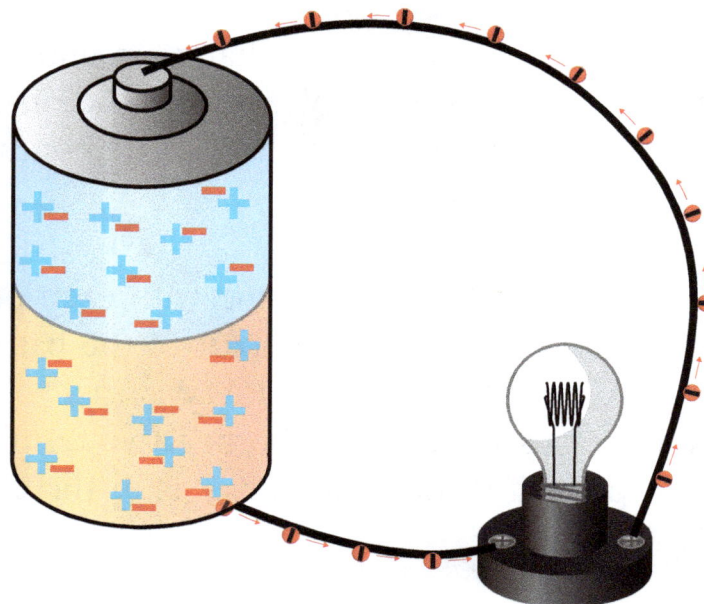

So a battery is one way to get electrons to move through a wire.

MAGNETS AND WIRES

Another way to get electrons to move in a wire is to move a magnet near a wire. You can also move a wire near a magnet. Remember how electrons move more easily through the metals used in wires? The magnet pushes or pulls the electrons.

This works whether you have a small magnet and thin wire or you have huge magnets and much thicker wires.

A device that produces electricity with magnets and wires is called a **generator**. A generator can be small enough to make enough electricity for only one home or big enough to supply it to a large area.

POWER STATIONS

Electricity is sometimes called **power.**

You may have heard the overhead electrical wires you see along roads called power lines.

A **power station** is a place where electricity is produced for a large area, like a state or even several states. In a power station there are usually several huge generators that change heat energy to electrical energy. Here's how this works.

1. Heat Energy

In the first section of the power station, a fuel is burned (for example, coal or oil). This makes heat energy. The heat energy from the burning fuel is used to make steam.

2. Motion Energy

As the steam is released, it turns a **turbine**, a large wheel with blades attached to it. This makes motion energy.

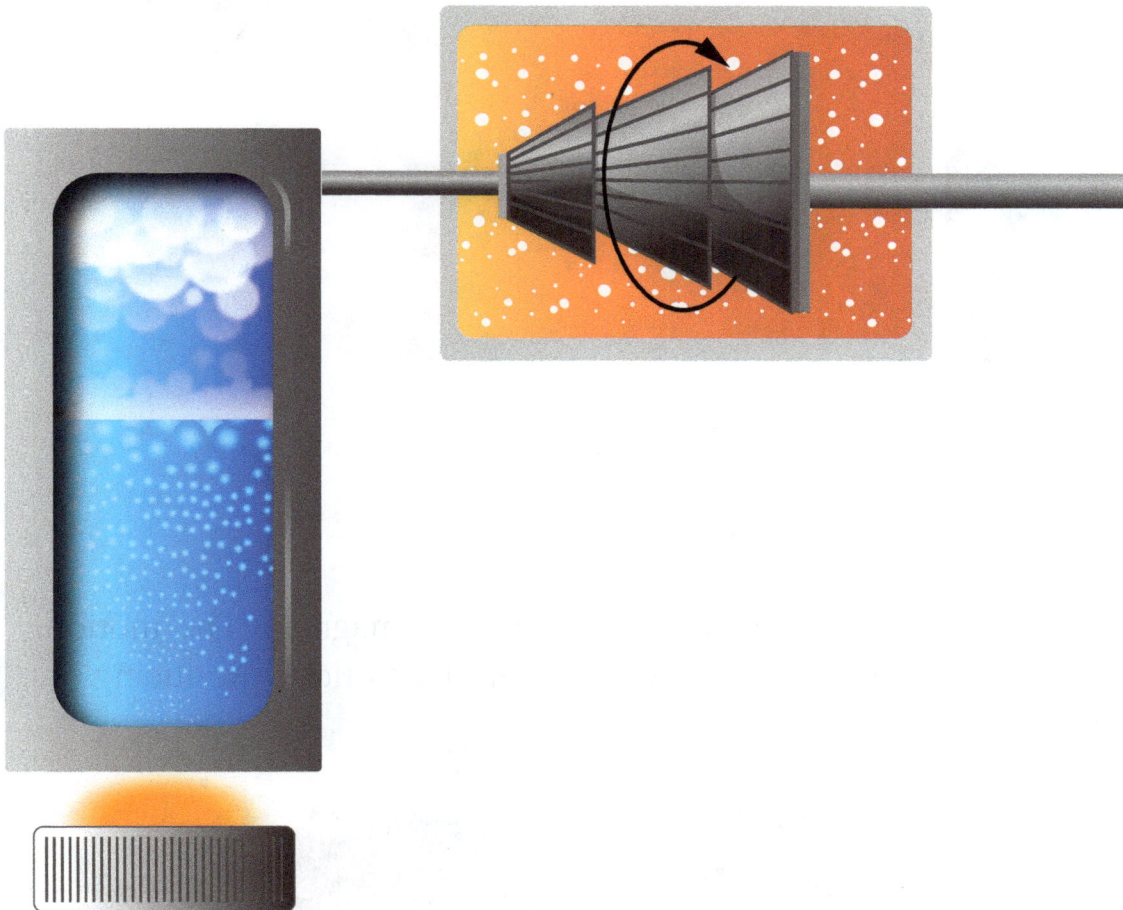

The turbine is attached to a shaft with a huge coil of wire at the other end. When the turbine turns, the wire coil turns.

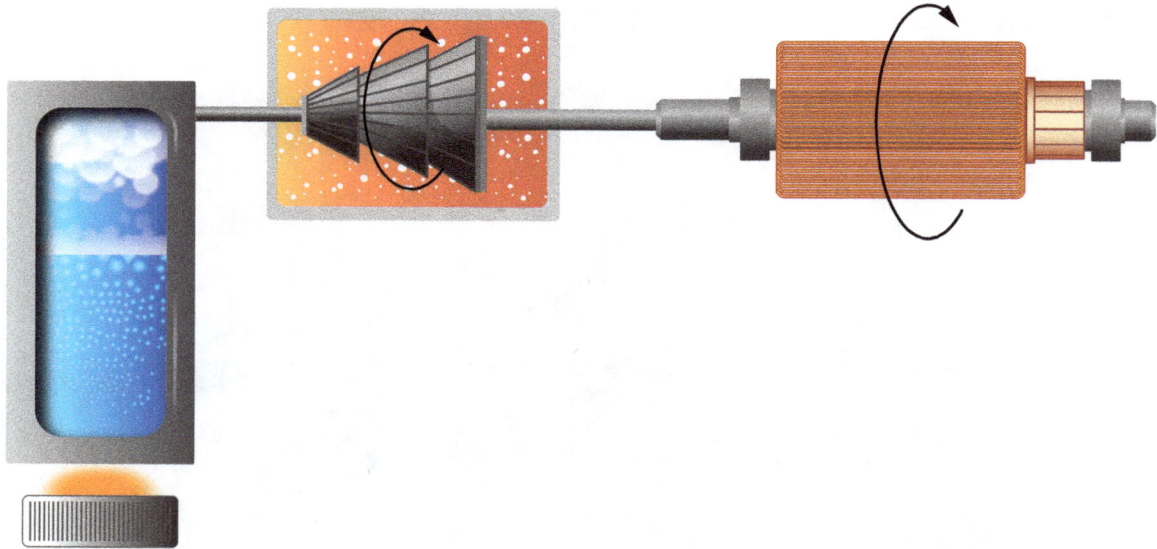

3. Electrical Energy

The wire spins inside a ring made of huge magnets. The motion of the wire near the magnets makes electrons flow, producing electrical energy.

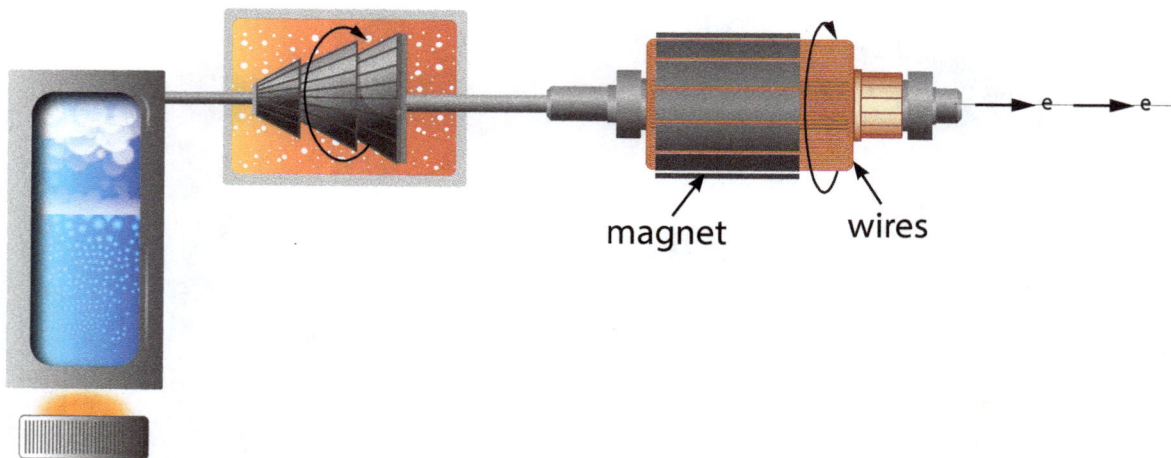

magnet   wires

The electricity flows out into long wires that go across the country and eventually connect to houses, schools, office buildings and all the other places that use electricity.

What started out as coal or oil has now resulted in a flow of electricity that can be used to make lights shine or washing machines run.

How Electricity Gets to You

7

After electricity is generated at a power station, it has to be sent to all the places where it will be used. This usually means getting the power across long distances to homes or businesses. Most power stations are hundreds of miles away from where the electricity they create is used.

STARTING OUT

The generators at a power station produce electricity that is about 200 times more powerful than the electricity you use in your home. But even so, it's not powerful enough to travel all the way from the power station to where you live. The problem is resistance.

Even though electricity moves through it easily, an electrical conductor still has some resistance. Its atoms tend to hold on to their electrons a bit, so even the free electrons have to be pushed or pulled along. In a very long wire, there can be a lot of resistance.

The electricity created in the power station has to have enough voltage to travel all the way to where it's going without being stopped by the resistance of the wire it's traveling through. But once it arrives, it has to be a low enough voltage to power things without damaging them.

The voltage of electricity can be changed to make it higher or lower. Very high voltage will get it from the power station to a city. Lower voltage will send it around the city to all the neighborhoods. An even lower voltage is what's used in homes and businesses.

CHANGING THE VOLTAGE

This is where a device called a transformer becomes useful. When something is **transformed**, it is changed into something different. For example, a caterpillar transforms into a butterfly. An **electrical transformer** is a device that changes electricity from one voltage to another. It transforms the voltage.

When a transformer changes electricity from low voltage to a higher voltage we say it has **stepped up** the voltage. When electricity is changed from high voltage to a lower voltage, we say it has been **stepped down**.

At a power station the electricity starts out at about 25,000 volts. Then transformers step up the voltage to between 155,000 volts and 765,000 volts—thousands of times more powerful than what is used in your home. This is the voltage that pushes the electricity through the many miles of power lines from the power station to where it will be used.

These are the power lines you may have seen on tall steel towers. The towers are called **pylons**.

It may seem odd, but these very high voltage wires don't have insulation around them. They are made of bare metal and are insulated in a different way.

The important thing is to keep the wires from touching the metal pylon since that would allow the high voltage electricity to pass into the pylon and then into the ground around the pylon. This would be dangerous to any people or animals touching the ground nearby.

To keep the high voltage wires away from the pylon, a set of insulators is used that looks like this.

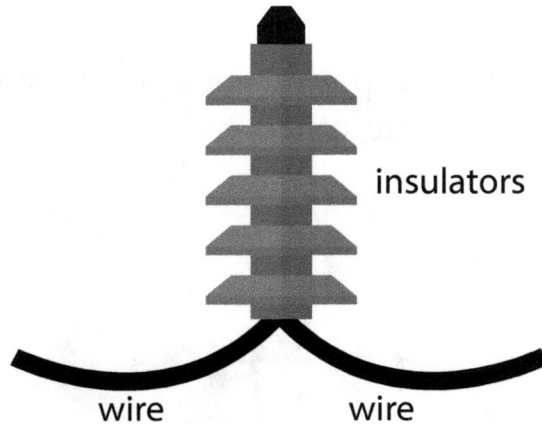

insulator

insulators

wire   wire

You can get an idea of how much voltage is in the wire by how many insulators are in the set. A lot of insulators means a lot of voltage.

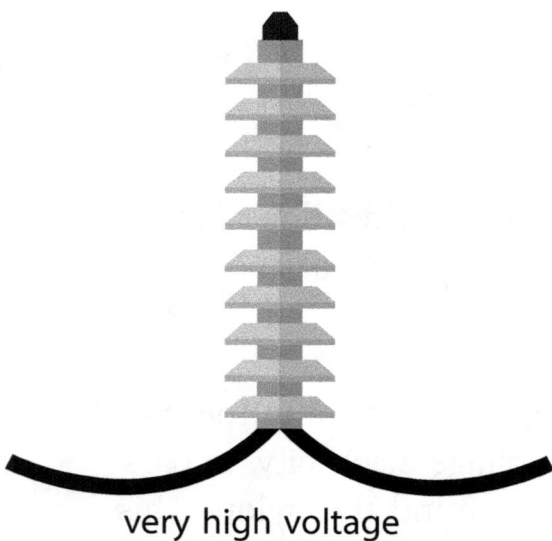

very high voltage   lower voltage   even lower voltage

STEPPING DOWN

When the electricity gets closer to where it will be used, it has to be stepped down to a lower voltage. This is done at a **sub-station.** The sub-station has transformers that step the 155,000 or 765,000 volts down to around 72,000 volts. This is still much higher than the voltage you use in your house. This is the voltage in the wires you may see on the wood power poles in your neighborhood. These wires are similar to the wires on the pylons. They are not covered with insulation and are kept away from the wood power poles by insulators. Since the voltage is lower, fewer insulators are needed.

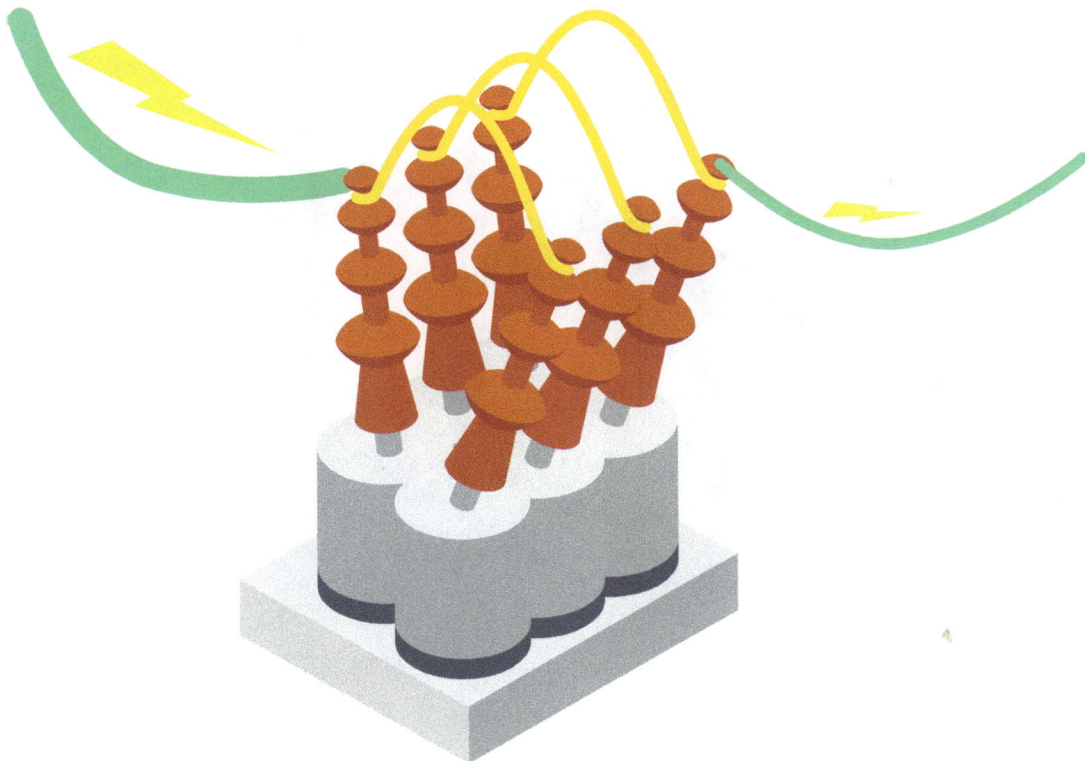

STEPPING DOWN AGAIN

To get the voltage down to what is used in your house, there is one more transformer. This transformer is on one of the power poles. It looks like a very large can. In fact, it is sometimes called a **can transformer**.

From this transformer the power goes to houses in the neighborhood. It is now at a voltage that can be used to power things in a home.

UNDERGROUND WIRES

In some cities and some newer neighborhoods, you will not see wires on power poles. The wires in these areas run underground where they are insulated and protected from weather and most accidents. Transformers for these wires look like large green or gray boxes. They are called **pad transformers** because they sit on a concrete platform called a pad.

POWER GRID

The whole network of wires that carry electrical power from a power plant to all the places it is used is called a **power distribution system** or **power grid**.

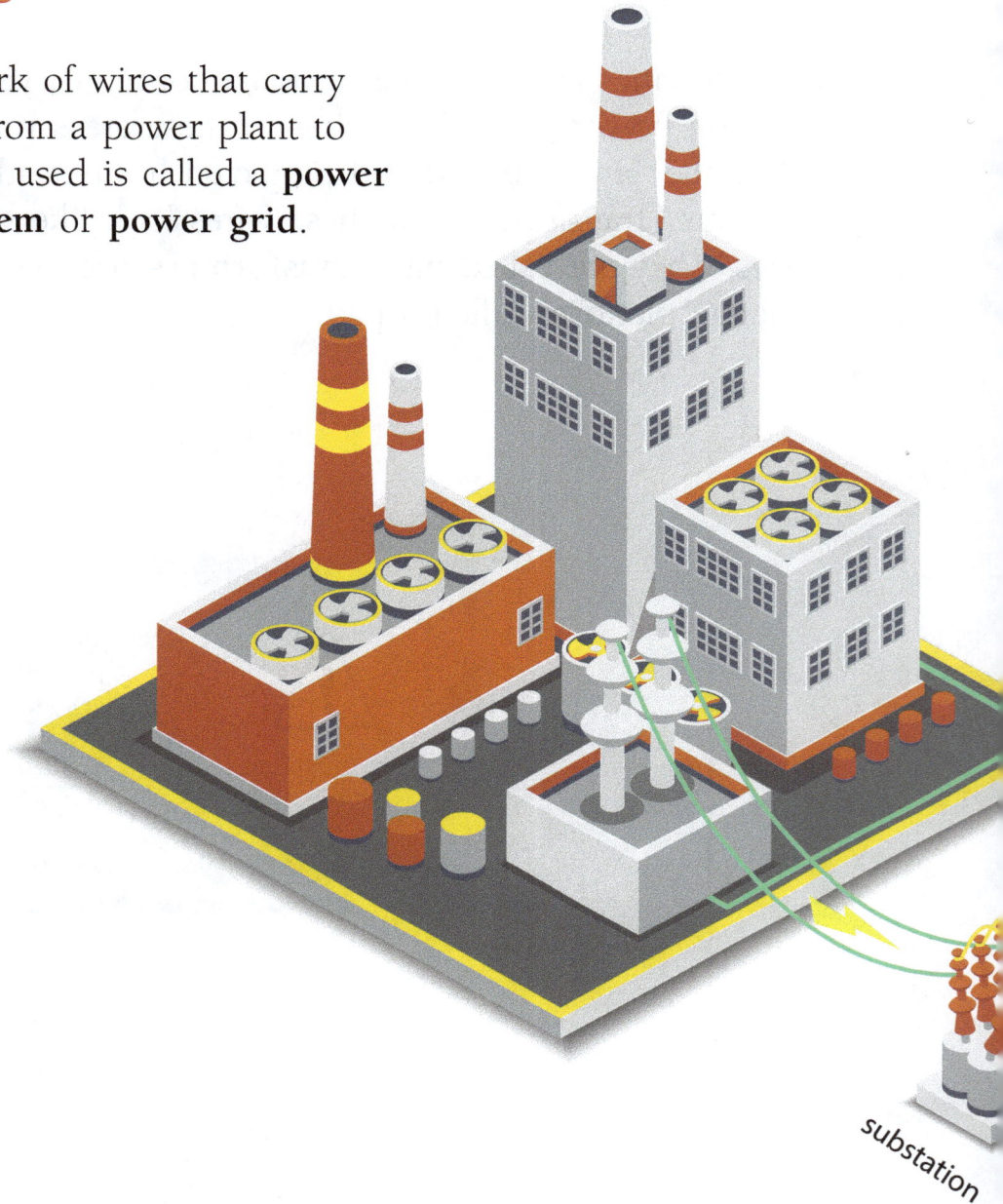

substation

It starts at a generator in a power plant, and goes through high-voltage power lines to a sub-station where the voltage is lowered and sent through local power lines with their transformers to houses and businesses.

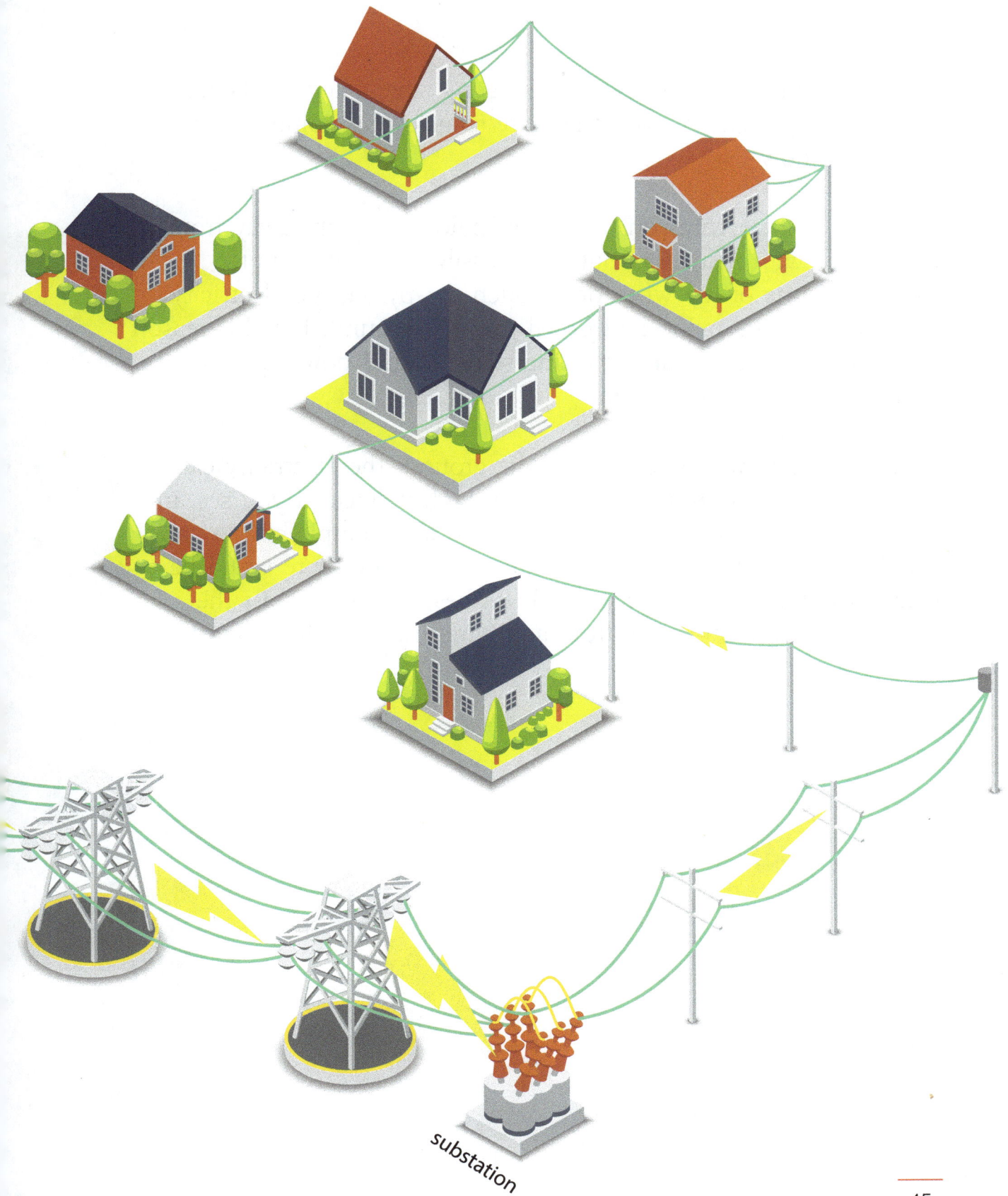

substation

SAFETY

Since so many of the wires you see along streets and roads are carrying very high voltages, there are some safety points it can be useful to know.

The high voltage wires on the power pylons are kept away from the pylons with insulators but it is possible for accidents to happen. If one of the wires does touch the pylon, the electricity can flow into the pylon and down into the ground. For this reason there are often fences and warning signs around power pylons. It's best to stay away from them.

If an outside power wire touches the ground, the electricity can flow into the ground at a dangerously high voltage. If you see an outside power wire touching the ground, for example after a car accident, stay away. Even if you don't see sparks, there could be electricity flowing into the ground. It's best to stay at least the length of a large bus away from any wire touching the ground.

ANIMALS ON THE WIRES

You may have seen birds or squirrels sitting or running on outdoor power lines. It may seem strange that they can do this without being hurt.

Here's how this works. For electrical current to hurt the animal, it has to pass *through* it to somewhere else. As long as an animal touches only one wire, the electrical current can't pass through the animal. For example, a bird sitting on a wire is safe as long as it touches only that one wire. If its wing touches another wire or the pylon, the current will pass through the bird, hurting it.

The same thing can happen to a person touching an uninsulated wire. Since it is almost impossible to touch a wire without touching something else at the same time, like the ground or a power pole, the best plan is not to touch wires at all.

Electricity in Your House

8

The electricity used in a house is supplied by an electric company (also called a power company) and is paid for according to the amount of electricity used.

How does the power company know how much to charge you? By measuring how much electricity is used.

A **meter** is a device that measures something. A water meter measures how much water is used in the house. A power meter, or electric meter, measures how much electricity is used. Electric companies use **electric meters** that constantly measure the current flowing into the house.

Any building that uses electricity will have an electric meter. You can usually find the electric meter for a house on the outside near where the power lines from the street connect to the building.

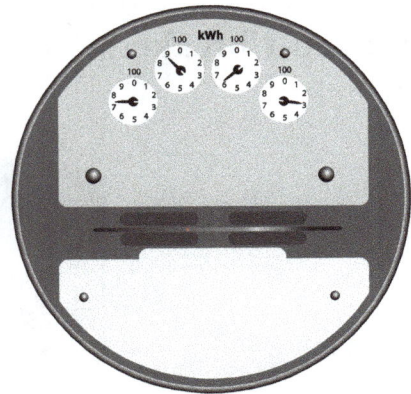

CIRCUIT BOX

On a wall inside a house, somewhere near where the power lines come into the house, there is a metal box called a **circuit box**.

Here the electricity coming into the house is divided up into separate circuits that go to different parts of the house.

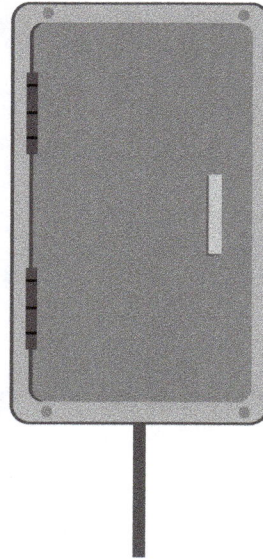

CIRCUIT BREAKERS

Each of these circuits goes through its own separate switch, called a **circuit breaker**. A circuit breaker looks like a very large light switch.

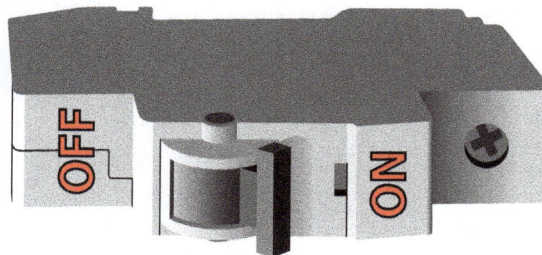

When the switch is in the "on" position, current can flow in the circuit. When it is in the "off" position, current can't flow. All the things that use electricity on that circuit stop working.

When an electrician needs to do work on the wires in a circuit, the breaker can be turned off. The electricity stops flowing in that circuit and the wires are safe to work with.

Another important job of a circuit breaker is to keep the current in each circuit from being too strong for the circuit to handle.

A circuit is designed to carry a certain amount of current, and the wires and insulation in the circuit are the right size for that amount. If more current flows through the wires, they could get hot and possibly melt, causing a fire.

If the current in a circuit goes above what it should be, its circuit breaker flips to a position halfway between "off" and "on." This breaks the circuit and stops the current.

This can happen when too many things are plugged into the circuit, causing too much current to flow.

MASTER SWITCH

At the very top of a circuit box, there is a switch much larger than the ones on the circuit breakers. This is called the **master switch**. A master switch is used to turn off all the circuits at once.

Circuits in Your House

The electrical circuits in your house provide power for lights, refrigerators, charging your cell phones and all the other things that need power. These circuits work differently than the very simple circuits you can build with a battery, wires and a few light bulbs.

When you use wires to connect a battery with a small light bulb, you create a circuit. The electricity comes from the battery, powers whatever is on the circuit, and flows back to the battery. If you add another light bulb to the circuit, the electricity flows in a line from the battery, through the first bulb, through the second bulb, then back to the battery.

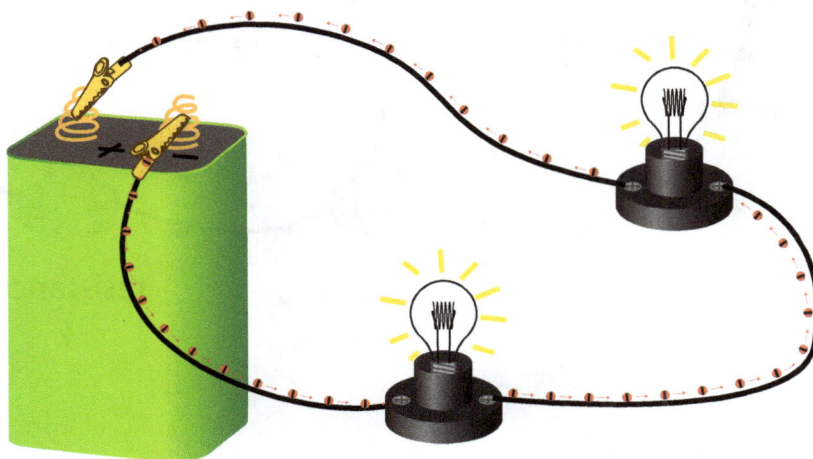

This is called a series circuit. A **series** is a number of similar things that follow each other in order, like a series of books. In a **series circuit**, all the electrons go through each device on the circuit in order, one after another.

The problem with this type of circuit is that if one device on the circuit stops working, the electrons can't pass through it to the next one. For example, if you remove one of the bulbs, the current can't flow to the next bulb and it won't shine.

Another problem with series circuits is resistance. Each device on a series circuit adds resistance to the circuit and lowers the current. If there are too many devices on the circuit, the resistance of all of them together lowers the current enough that none of the devices get as much as they need. One light bulb connected to a battery can shine brightly. Three or four bulbs will be dim or won't shine at all unless you add another battery.

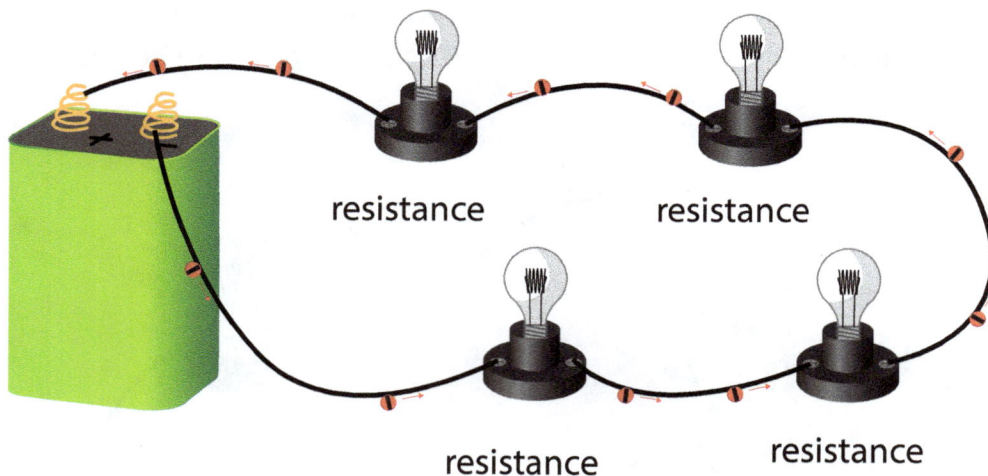

resistance   resistance

resistance   resistance

There is a way to create a circuit that doesn't have these problems.

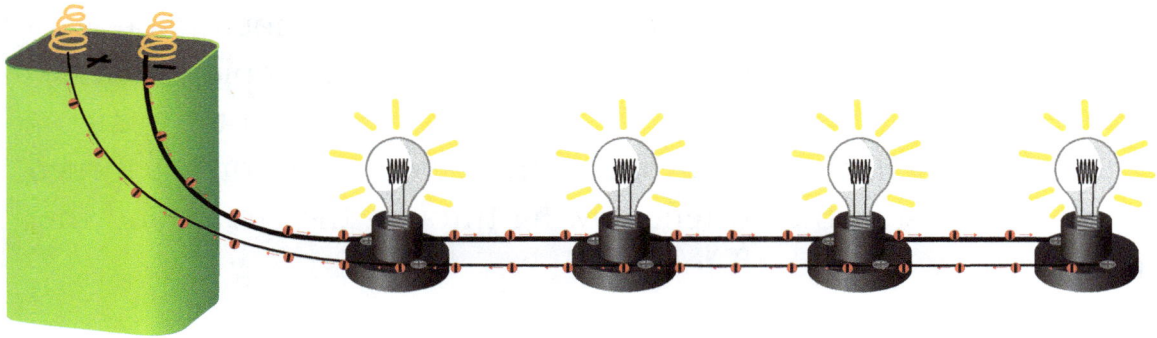

If you connect the wires like this, the electrons can flow all the way through the circuit even if a bulb is missing or not working.

The electrons come into the circuit from the battery. Some of the electrons go through the first light bulb and make it shine. Some of the electrons go past the first bulb and go through the second bulb making it shine. Both bulbs get enough current to shine brightly. Each gets all the power it needs, and if one stops working, it doesn't affect the other one.

This kind of circuit is called a **parallel circuit** because the wires go along side by side. They are not exactly the same distance apart all the time (as parallel lines are) but they are side by side.

HOUSE CIRCUITS

You can probably imagine that if the circuits in a house were series circuits, there would be a lot of problems. For example, in your living room you might have two lamps plugged in to the same circuit. In a series circuit, if one of the lamps broke or got turned off, it would stop the current flowing through the circuit and the other lamp would go off too.

To keep this from happening the circuits for outlets and lights in a house are parallel circuits. Here's how they work.

Each circuit has a wire that brings current into the circuit. This is called the "hot" wire. It has black or red insulation.

And each circuit has a wire that brings current back to the circuit box. This is called the "neutral" wire. It has white insulation.

Together they make a full circuit. Each circuit has several outlets that it supplies power to. For each of these outlets there is a wire that brings the current into the outlet or light and one that allows the current to flow back to the circuit breaker box.

Here's how a circuit for a living room might look:

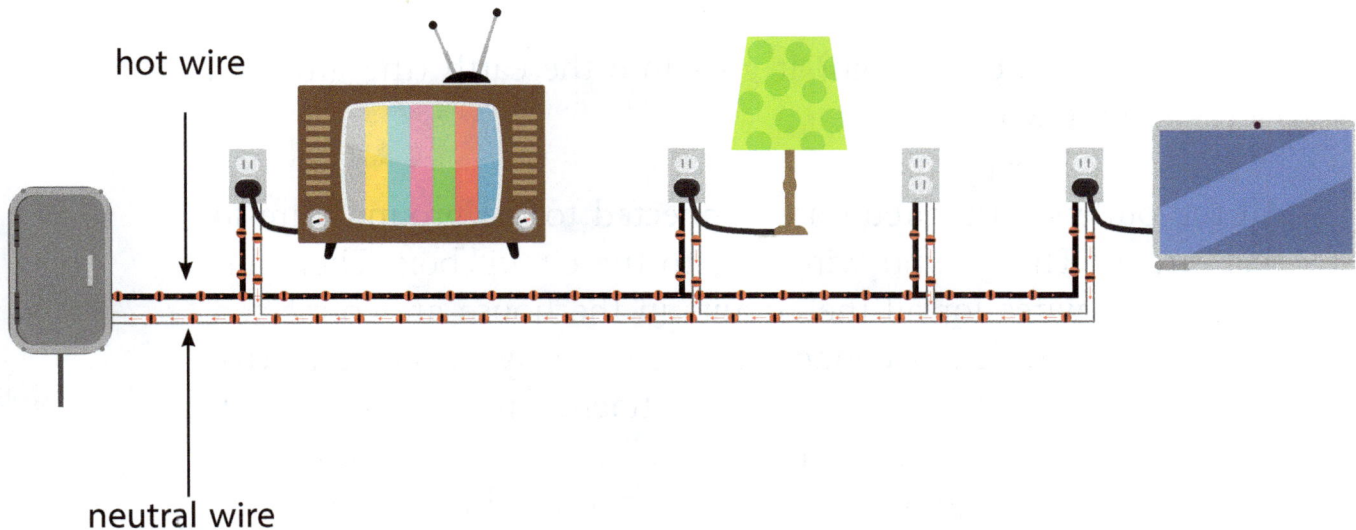

hot wire

neutral wire

Each device gets all the current it needs.

SAFETY GROUND

When a circuit and all the devices on it are working as they should, the electricity flows from the circuit breaker box, through each of the devices and back to the box. All the electricity stays where it belongs.

But what would happen if there was a broken wire in the circuit or in one of the outlets on it? Electricity could flow where it doesn't belong. We need a way to keep this from happening.

In addition to the hot wire and the neutral wire, most circuits have another wire called the **ground wire**. This wire is either bare copper or covered with green insulation. The ground wire is there to make sure that if there is a problem anywhere in the circuit, the current has somewhere safe to go.

Where does the current go? It goes into the earth (the ground). Here's how it works.

All the outlets on a circuit are connected to the ground wire for that circuit. The ground wire goes to the circuit box. There all the ground wires for all the circuits in the house are connected to a larger wire that is connected in some way to the earth (the ground). The ground wire could be attached to a metal pipe that goes underground, or it could be attached to a metal rod that is pounded into the ground outside the house. This is called the **safety ground** (or simply **ground**).

The voltage going from the safety ground into the earth is not dangerously high. It is much less than the voltage in an outdoor power wire.

A COMPLETE CIRCUIT

A complete circuit for a room might look like this:

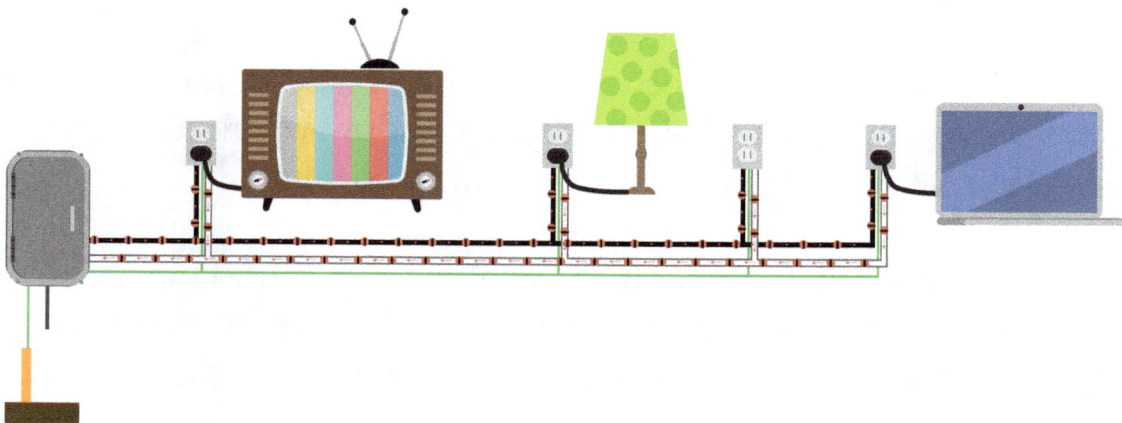

Outlets and Plugs

10

You have probably seen that most electrical outlets in your house have two slots and a hole.

The rectangular slot on the right is slightly shorter than the one on the left. This is where the hot wire (the wire that brings the current) is attached. The longer slot on the left is where the neutral wire (the wire that carries the current away) is attached. The hole on the bottom is where the ground wire is attached.

Here are some plugs you may have seen around your house.

The metal pieces that stick out of the plug are called **prongs**. Most plugs have two prongs. Other plugs have three prongs, two for the slots and a rounder prong for the ground wire hole. This type of plug is used for devices that need to be connected to the safety ground wire.

If you look around your house, you can probably find examples of both kinds of plugs.

Everyday Electricity

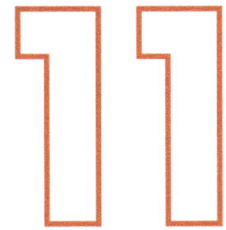

11

Electricity is a big part of our everyday life. It powers everything from tiny flashlights, cell phones, lamps and computers, to huge air conditioners big enough to cool an indoor stadium.

Making electrons move, and go where we want them to go, makes it possible to do all these things and more!

Appendix

GLOSSARY

A

atom: one of the very, very tiny pieces that matter is made of. Atoms are made of protons, neutrons and electrons. (Chapters 1 and 2)

attract: When one thing is attracted by another thing, it pulls towards it. (Chapter 2)

C

can transformer: a transformer that looks like a very large can attached to a power pole. Can transformers bring the electricity in the power distribution system down to a voltage that can be used in a building. (Chapter 7)

charge: another word for electrical energy. (Chapter 6)

chemical: a material that causes a change in another material when they are combined. (Chapter 6)

circuit: A circuit is a loop or path that comes back to the same place it starts out. (Chapter 4)

circuit box: This is where the electricity coming into a building is divided up into separate circuits that go to different parts of the building. (Chapter 8)

circuit breaker: A circuit breaker looks like a very large light switch. When the switch is in the "on" position, current can flow in the circuit. When it is in the "off" position, current can't flow. (Chapter 8)

conductor: a material that allows electrons to pass through. (Chapter 3)

E

electric current: the flow of electrons through a conductor. (Chapter 3)

electric meter: a device that measures how much electricity is used in a building. (Chapter 8)

electrical circuit: a path for electrons that starts somewhere, for example at a battery, and makes a complete loop back to where it started. (Chapter 4)

electrical force: the pushing and pulling that happens between the particles in an atom. The pull between an electron and a proton. The push between two electrons or two protons. (Chapter 2)

electrical transformer: a device that changes electricity from one voltage to another. (Chapter 7)

electron: a tiny particle that moves around the nucleus of an atom. Electrons are negative. (Chapter 2)

electricity: the movement of electrons. (Chapter 3)

F

force: a push or pull, no matter how weak or strong. (Chapter 2)

free electron: an electron that can get away from its nucleus and move from one atom to another. (Chapter 2)

G

generator: a device that produces electricity with magnets and wires. (Chapter 6)

ground wire: a wire in a circuit that is there to make sure that if there is a problem in a circuit, the electricity has somewhere safe to go. (Chapter 9)

I

insulator: a material that does not allow electrons to move around freely. (Chapter 3)

M

master switch: a switch at the top of a circuit box that can be used to turn off all the circuits at once. It is much larger than the circuit breaker switches. (Chapter 8)

matter: all the things that make up the world around us. Matter is made up of atoms. (Chapter 1)

meter: a device that measures something. A power meter, or electric meter, measures how much electricity is used in a house or other building. (Chapter 8)

N

natural law: a statement about how things act in nature (Chapter 4)

neutron: a tiny particle in the nucleus of an atom. A neutron is neither negative nor positive. (Chapter 2)

nucleus: the center of an atom, made of protons and neutrons. (**Nuclei** is plural of nucleus.) (Chapter 2)

O

outlet: the place where you plug in a wire for a device that runs on electricity. (Chapter 5)

P

pad transformer: In some cities and neighborhoods, the wires run underground. The transformers for these wires look like large green or gray boxes. They are called pad transformers because they sit on a concrete platform called a pad. (Chapter 7)

parallel circuit: a circuit put together so that each device in the circuit gets enough current to work well. A parallel circuit looks like this:

(Chapter 9)

particle: a tiny part of something. In an atom the particles are protons, neutrons and electrons. (Chapter 2)

power: electricity is sometimes called power. (Chapter 6)

power distribution system: the whole network of wires that carry electricity from a power plant to all the places it is used. (Chapter 7)

power grid: another name for a power distribution system. (Chapter 7)

power station: a place where electricity is produced for a large area, like a state or even several states. (Chapter 6)

prong: the metal pieces that stick out of the plug are called prongs. (Chapter 10)

proton: a tiny particle in the nucleus of an atom. A proton is positive. (Chapter 2)

pylon: one of the tall steel towers that carry high voltage wires.

R

repel: When one thing is repelled by another thing, it pushes away from it. (Chapter 2)

resistance: When electrons can't move freely through something (like a light bulb), they are slowed down. This slowing down of the electrons is called resistance. (Chapter 4)

S

safety ground: the ground wires for all the circuits in a building are connected to a larger wire that is connected in some way to the earth (the ground). It could be attached to a metal pipe that goes underground or it could be attached to a metal rod that is pounded into the ground outside the house. This is called the safety ground, or simply ground. (Chapter 9)

series: a number of similar things that follow each other in order. (Chapter 9)

series circuit: a circuit put together so that all the electrons go through each device on the circuit in order, one after another. A series circuit looks like this:

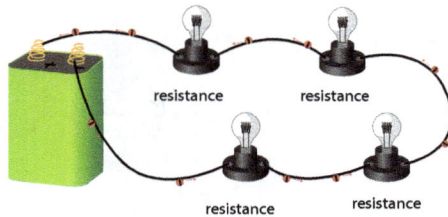

(Chapter 9)

short circuit: a circuit in which the electrons flow too quickly, with nothing to slow them down. A short circuit can happen when uninsulated or broken wires touch. (Chapter 4)

stepped down: When a transformer changes electricity from high voltage to a lower voltage, we say it has been stepped down. (Chapter 7)

stepped up: When a transformer changes electricity from low voltage to a higher voltage, we say it has been stepped up. (Chapter 7)

strand: something that looks like a thread. A very thin wire that looks like a thread is called a strand. (Chapter 5)

stranded wire: wire made of many strands twisted together. All of the strands together act as a single conductor. (Chapter 5)

sub-station: a place in a power distribution system where high voltage is stepped down to a lower voltage. (Chapter 7)

switch: a device in a circuit that can be closed to let electrons flow through the circuit and opened to stop the flow. When the switch is open, there is a gap in the circuit and the electrons can't flow. (Chapter 4)

T

terminal: a place on a battery where a wire can be connected. (Chapter 4)

transform: to change into something different. (Chapter 7)

turbine: a large wheel with blades attached to it. The wheel can be turned by water, steam or air passing through the blades. (Chapter 6)

V

volt: the unit for measuring voltage. (Chapter 5)

voltage: the amount of push moving electrons through a circuit; how hard the electrons are being pushed or pulled along. (Chapters 4 and 5)

Everyday Electricity

Book

Everyday Electricity, Heron Books

Other Materials

- [ ] *Everyday Electricity Teacher Tips,* Heron Books (downloadable)
- [ ] Balloons (9 to 12 inch)
- [ ] String
- [ ] Aluminum foil
- [ ] White vinegar
- [ ] Plastic ice cube tray
- [ ] Small Styrofoam balls (1- to 2-inch diameter)
- [ ] Fine grade sandpaper
- [ ] Six alligator clip leads (6-12 inch length)
- [ ] Two 6-volt lantern batteries with coil spring terminals
- [ ] Two 6-volt miniature light bulbs—screw-in type (also called lamp board bulbs)
- [ ] Two sockets for 6-volt bulbs (also called bulb holders)
- [ ] Several 12-volt motors designed to run on batteries
- [ ] One single blade knife switch
- [ ] Samples of wire used to carry electricity (14-gauge solid conductor house wire, stranded wire lamp cord or extension cord, low voltage single conductor bell wire, headphone wire, other wire samples as available)

- [ ] Circuit breaker (not installed in a panel)
- [ ] Uninsulated 18-gauge copper wire
- [ ] Enamel insulated 18-gauge copper wire
- [ ] Five galvanized nails (1 to 1 ½ inch)
- [ ] LED bulb (any color)
- [ ] Galvanometer
- [ ] Three-inch-long bolt
- [ ] Magnet (rectangular ceramic type)
- [ ] Transformer with 120 volts AC on the input side and 12 volts AC on the output side that can be plugged into a wall outlet. (This allows the student to test input and output voltages without changing from AC to DC on the voltmeter.)
- [ ] A simple voltmeter with digital readout
- [ ] Hand-crank generator designed for kids. It should have a built-in bulb and terminals where alligator clip leads can be attached. It should allow the student to see the gears and motor clearly. Examples: United Scientific Supplies Hand Held Generator from Fisherscic.com or Hand Held Manual Electricity DC Crank Generator (light bulb kit) from Banggood.com
- [ ] A small motor that's been opened

SUBSCRIBER SCHOOLS

Delphian School®
K-12 boarding and day
20950 SW Rock Creek Rd
Sheridan, OR 97378
503.843.3521
delphian.org

Delphi Academy®
of Los Angeles
PreK-12 day
11341 Brainard Ave
Lake View Terrace, CA 91342
818.583.1070
delphila.org

Delphi Academy
of Boston
PreK-8 day
564 Blue Hill Ave
Milton, MA 02186
617.333.9610
delphiboston.org

Delphi Academy
of Florida
PreK-12 day
1831 Drew St
Clearwater, FL 33765
727.447.6385
delphifl.org

Oak Crest
Private School
PreK-8 day
1200 E Jackson Rd, Bldg 2
Carrollton, TX 75006
214.483.5400
oakcrestschool.org

Delphi Academy
of Campbell
K-8 day
One West Campbell Ave., Building A
Campbell, CA 95008
408.370.7400
delphicampbell.org

Ability School
PreK-8 day
75 Knickerbocker Rd
Englewood, NJ 07631
201.871.8808
abilityschoolnj.com

Whether kindergarten through 3rd, 6th, 8th or 12th grade, subscriber schools license with Heron Books to use the DELPHI PROGRAM™ which includes a comprehensive curriculum and structure designed to encourage every student to reason, to think creatively, to look at the world independently, and to evaluate information for its relative importance and usefulness. To see the Delphi Program in action, visit any of the above subscriber schools. For information on subscriber school services and materials, email info@heronbooks.com.